# GILT FREE

# GILT FREE

## DITCHING YOUR GILDED CAGE FOR GOOD

KEREN ELDAD

# Praise for *GILT FREE*

"The long-awaited sequel to Keren Eldad's *GILDED* is here, and it's everything you've been waiting for. *GILT FREE* takes us into new territory, beyond what I call the Upper Limit Problem, providing a map to a land many people are exploring today."

– GAY HENDRICKS, AUTHOR OF *THE BIG LEAP*

"This book is a map leading to the eternal treasure: self-understanding, purpose, and alignment. Drawn by one who pioneered the route and has guided many others across tricky terrain, it is brilliantly written—obstacles and opportunities made crystal clear. Realistic but optimistic, it is not for those looking for a few affirmations and a pat on the head. It is for those who have hit the wall and know there must be a more aligned way to live the rest of their life."

– ASHA NAYASWAMI

"In *GILT FREE*, Keren Eldad offers a powerful invitation to step out of the gilded cages we often build for ourselves in the pursuit of success. With insight, candor, and compassion, she reveals how overachievement can quietly disconnect us from our true selves—and how reclaiming honesty, integrity, and self-belonging can lead to a far more meaningful life."

–DR. KRISTIN NEFF, AUTHOR, *SELF-COMPASSION* AND
*FIERCE SELF-COMPASSION*

"*GILT FREE* is a reclamation. Keren guides us out of the gilded cage of "having it all" and into the deeper, richer truth of living in integrity with our soul. This book is for the woman who is ready to start fully inhabiting her one precious life."

– JESSICA ZWEIG, BESTSELLING AUTHOR OF *BE.* AND *THE LIGHT WORK*

"A masterpiece in identity shifts and who you could become, Keren articulates beautifully how to stretch to new limits and soften your grip to accelerate your manifestation. The perfect blend of spirituality and practicality, this is a must read."
– CRAIG SIEGEL, WSJ BESTSELLING AUTHOR, CPC COACH, TEACHER, TEDX SPEAKER, 9X MARATHONER, AND INVESTOR

"KEREN has truly done it again! With wit and precision, *GILT FREE* gives not only language but practical solutions to the burnt-out, over-efforting high-achievers who know there's a better way to live. Helping you move from a life secretly driven by control, fear, and scarcity, to one of alignment, truth, and peace. She breaks down the radical blocks standing in our way and offers a framework to find our golden path home."
– JESSICA GILL, *TO BE MAGNETIC*

"In *GILT FREE*, Eldad gives us a brisk, funny, and heartfelt guide to freeing ourselves from seeking external validation and coming to live instead from the bedrock truth of our own inner authority. The life-changing reframes in Eldad's work are grounded in both her own hard-won experience, her sensitive understanding of Jungian psychological integration, and her brilliant coaching work with top-tier clients from around the world.

If you're a high-achieving person who's tired of chasing accolades and who wants to find genuine fulfillment instead, you need to stop what you're doing right now and give yourself the gift of reading *GILT FREE*."
– DR. CAROLYN ELLIOTT, AUTHOR OF *EXISTENTIAL KINK* AND *AWAKEN YOUR GENIUS*

"*People only get really interesting when they start to rattle the bars of their cages.*"
ALAIN DE BOTTON

Headshot Photography: Shanaz Maharaj

Keren Eldad
*Gilt Free* by Keren Eldad — 1st ed.

Paperback ISBN: 979-8-9937986-4-6
Hardcover ISBN: 979-8-9937986-5-3

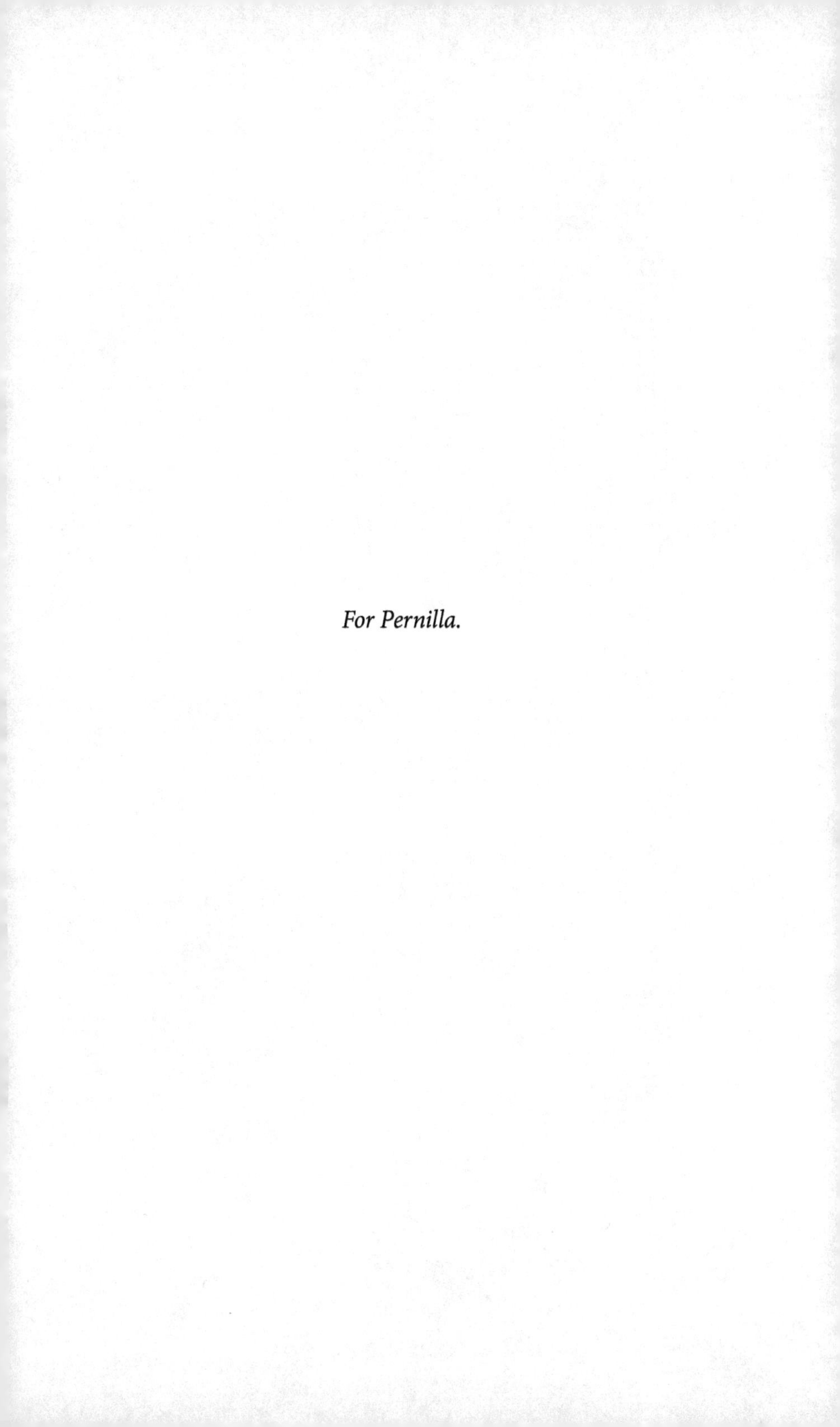

*For Pernilla.*

# Contents

# INTRODUCTION

*"There's a wonderful quote that's attributed to George Lucas:
'We are all living in cages with the door wide open.' That was me until I realized I had the power—and the responsibility—to set myself
free. To step out of the cage of whatever I'd experienced in the past,
to think for myself, and to believe in my choices."*

INA GARTEN

*I*t is a truth universally accepted that those who achieve the most will end
*up the happiest.* Whether this happiness survives close examination is
another matter entirely. In fact, this "truth" may be the greatest lie of modern life: If you get the grades, chase the right job, marry well, make some
money, decorate the house, and hit the prescribed milestones, fulfillment
will inevitably follow.

You and I both know the real truth by now. You can do all of this—
check every box, play every part perfectly—and still feel like you're
drowning. Which renders success a moot point. Because success without freedom isn't success at all. It's a cage. Gilded, perhaps. But a cage
nonetheless.

Consuelo Vanderbilt (yes, a member of the Vanderbilt family) knew
this better than anyone. At the height of America's Gilded Age—1895—
she was one of the richest young women in the country and had been
raised as such, not to live, but to perform and to uphold the very gilded
cage into which she had been born. Let me summarize the early part of
her bio for you: From childhood on, every move was choreographed by
her ambitious mother, Alva Vanderbilt. Alva made Consuelo wear posture braces at night, taught her strict, perfect manners by day, and when

Consuelo came "of age," Alva allowed absolutely no suitors except ones with prestigious titles.

And it worked. At seventeen, she was married off to a duke in a wedding that made headlines around the world. To the press and the very rich society of New York, it looked like she had won the ultimate prize. On the streets of Manhattan, thousands cheered her carriage, which symbolized American money securing a European title. What they did not see was that inside the carriage sat a young woman being marched into a life where her voice would not be required, giving serious Marie-Antoinette-going-to-the-guillotine vibes. What she "won" was loneliness alongside a husband who could not have cared less about her, who only married her for the money, and who was about to whisk her away across the ocean to a freezing, dilapidated castle, and to a life that belonged to her even less than the one she was departing.

For years, Consuelo endured this new, empty life, living isolated in the duke's frozen home, Blenheim Palace. She smiled, did what was expected, and made her life performance flawless. Read her memoir, *The Glitter and the Gold*, and you can hear the training still humming beneath Consuelo's prose. Her writing is composed, dignified, nearly austere in its restraint, because that's how Consuelo Vanderbilt was taught to behave. In that book, Consuelo describes those days as a life of bowing, curtsying, and being walked back into line, even though all she wanted was something as human as holding her own child a minute longer before a nanny took him away.

In time, Consuelo found the courage to do something epochal: She stopped. Having reached her own limit, Consuelo separated from the duke in 1906, and though the formal annulment would come much later, the severing began the very day she chose herself. In so doing, Consuelo risked it all, walking away from a palace and from a vast fortune—not to make a statement but to make a life.

A life is precisely what she made. From then on, Consuelo Vanderbilt became not only an author, but a tireless activist—championing women's suffrage, patronizing hospitals and relief efforts, and showing up not merely with a signature on a check, but with her sleeves rolled up, ready to do the work. Even her mother, Alva, who had all but engineered the arrangement, eventually transformed upon witnessing her daughter's undeniable evolution and joy throwing herself into the suffrage movement and later supporting Consuelo's annulment, publicly admitting her coercion. The philanthropic causes she championed during two world wars weren't penance; they were expression and the natural generosity of a person re-inhabiting her true self.

The irony was delicious and instructive: The marriage that had been a cold bargain became a doorway to a conscience. There is grace in that arc—coercion to contrition to repair. It does not undo the harm, but it does model that liberation can ripple into what we all truly want: fulfillment.

What happened there, with Consuelo? People like me would say she found courage—and we would be right. But there's another name for it, one that belongs to psychology and describes the inner journey that Consuelo undoubtedly undertook: individuation, Carl Jung's word for the long, spiraling journey of becoming who you are, not who you were trained to be. It is the movement away from the persona (the mask you wear for approval and belonging) toward the Self (the integrated center that can hold your shadow and your light without collapsing). It is the privilege of a lifetime, Jung wrote (how I love that quote!). It is also, let's be honest, the fight of a lifetime.

Belonging to ourselves is a noble cause. Consuelo's story serves to illustrate that, yes, this rise is possible. It also serves as caution that the project of coming to belong to oneself—for people with a lot to lose—is a fight. For those entrenched in societies and familial expectations, the external world rewards the masks worn, the continued assimilation, the "fitting in," and loves a polished persona that hits the marks, smiles on cue, and doesn't make anyone uncomfortable by insisting on having a real soul (how else would you explain Instagram?). It rewards obedience, good taste, curated images, and, eventually, causes us to be vigilant—never letting the mask slip. In time, we can become confused about the difference between applause and obsequiousness with alignment, and the longer we perform, the harder it becomes to remember where the performance ends and our true self begins.

I roped us into this situation because living as a performance isn't just the problem of duchesses, it's the modern condition. You don't need a mother like Alva to push you into a posture brace. You've got an algorithm. You don't need a duke to lock you in a castle. You've got a calendar full of commitments you never consciously chose. The gilded cage is less obvious now, making it more dangerous. It doesn't clang when it closes. It whispers, "good job."

## MY GILDED STORY

My cage wasn't built in Blenheim Palace. My cage was assembled over many years, growing ever shinier with each "good job" and gold star. It started in elementary-school classrooms where scratch-and-sniff stickers were awarded for a grade of 95% and above (A+), and chocolate cake was awarded for winning spelling bees. I will never forget the day I inhaled the synthetic strawberry scent of a Strawberry Shortcake sticker and felt a jolt of worth flood my small body. Or the first time *I won the cake*. Those moments were the moments that imprinted on my mind, setting a path. From those early dopamine hits, I never wanted to be average again; I stayed at the top of the honor list. I didn't know that excellence, pursued without the ballast of self, can be yet another addiction. That, it certainly is.

That addiction has a name: overachiever. It consists of uncontrollable behaviors like control, anxious overthinking, perfectionism, and obsessive work habits.

In case those behaviors do not speak to you, when I say "overachiever," here's who I'm talking about in these pages: *Overachiever, or high achiever (used interchangeably),* doesn't just mean valedictorians, CEOs, or Olympic hopefuls, though they (you?) are very welcome here. It means anyone capable of intense focus who channels that drive into doing *more* than achieving. Overachievers aren't defined by résumés or titles; they're defined by their relationship to effort, striving, fixing, perfecting, optimizing, and doing more than is necessary—often at the expense of ease and self-care. They can be executives, parents, artists, or gardeners: anyone who takes their endeavors a little too far. *Healthy achievers*, by contrast, apply focus to meaningful goals and can rest in "enough." Overachievers keep trying long after "enough" has been reached.

From a very young age, I fell into the unhealthy category. And I firmly stayed there until my mid-thirties. Decades passed where I did everything "right." As I did, my cage grew more and more confining. After high school, joining the Israeli army was what my parents preferred for me—*before* university—as was mandated by the state, so off I went. Then, when I finally went to university, regaining my A+ accolades, I did so while bartending, because hustle is holy and why not work *all* the time?

Graduation was followed by a swift move to New York City, where all top achievers go, right? And then came *The-Devil-Wears-Prada* decade: my first career, in publishing, with all the fashion, the status, the names, the undereating, and the dating horrors. During that time, I stacked up achievements like a child stacking up toy blocks—half-terrified of anyone noticing that fear, not joy, was holding the tower together.

Then, at the age of 30, I finally did the biggest "right" thing: I managed to marry the "right" man by the rules of the wrong life. He was tall (sort of), worked in banking, and checked all the main boxes (basically, just those two). Marriage was the crown jewel according to my overachieving logic; it fit the persona perfectly and starved the person entirely. Sensing rebellion in my psyche (I've always been a low-key smart-aleck), he quickly convinced me to leave the city I loved for a city that did not know me: Zurich.

Zurich is punctual, polite, and gray. In the two years I lived there, every day felt like death, only slower. I don't mean the fine people of Zurich any disrespect, but I do totally and unapologetically want you to know that what I personally found there was a lifestyle as misaligned to my soul as a tropical environment would be to a penguin. To paraphrase Boney M. (now *there's* an old-school reference you will need to look up): *I wept, as I remembered Zion.*

For years, I endured performing this role while posting plenty of pictures on social media to uphold the image of "I'm super, thanks for asking." I curated an illusion. "Look how awesome my life is" was written by my choices. Every month, there was another gala, another trip to Milan, another matched look, another caption-performing "partnership" that was, in truth, abdication, of finances ("fine, *you* handle it"), of needs ("it's not that important"), of voice ("why fight?"), of self ("just be easy").

At work, I was almost as pathetic. For two years, I grossly undersold myself and hid from promotions—the holy sacrament of the high-achieving self-erasure. Suddenly okay with what was clearly a demotion from my days in New York City, I called my situation "humility" when it was actually fear and called it "stability" when it was instead stagnation. In this suspended state, I even called my grief "gratuitous." Which was how it ended up almost killing me. Literally.

After *two whole years* in that wretched Blenheim Palace-esque town, we moved apartments and, on that one, fateful moving day, my personal belongings were stolen. *My* things were stolen—not *ours*, not *his*. Next, we had to file a police report, and once we did that, my would-be-ex-husband was forced to make an admission to me: He had never paid our insurance premiums. Months and months of *"I'll handle it,"* and, it turns out, *nothing was handled.*

Over the coming days, the quicksand revealed itself; the finances I had "handed over" were not in any grown-up sense being managed at all. Also, I *had grown to detest* that guy, repulsed by his increasingly erratic and cruel behavior toward me, which only became more intolerable in the aftermath of such an overt mess up. By the time of the great robbery, I was already sleeping in a separate room, following two years of his emotionally-abusive behavior toward me. Yet, it took this disillusionment for me to come face to face with the truth: Not only was this marriage terrible, but the entire life I had been propping up with optics was a complete sham.

Anyway, I got out of there. It was *brutal*, but I got out of that gilded cage.

## THE INTEGRITY LINE

There's a particular sound your soul makes when it realizes the depth of its own self-betrayal. Mine made that sound—a sort of howling—in a shower at the end of that week, while ABBA's "My Love, My Life" played loudly and drowned out my sobs. As I cried, this thought came barreling in: "If this is where I have ended up in life, I'm not sure I want it. Maybe I should just end this now." That's what I thought.

Luckily, something larger than my panic—call it grace, God, guardian angels, or simply the last unextinguished pilot light of self—kept me standing long enough to get out of that shower and realize that I did not actually want to die.

In that moment, I got a second truth. **What I wanted to kill was not me—it was *the performance*.** I had been blocked, like so many overachievers before me and since, by a persona that had outlived its usefulness. Blocked by the oldest lies in the world ("If you behave, they will love you." "If you achieve, you will be celebrated." "If you are humble, no one will punish you."). Blocked by the gilded bars of success without freedom. That night didn't end my pain, but it did end my denial.

That night nearly cost me my life, and is why I do what I do, and why I wrote my previous book, *Gilded*. I don't want you, or anyone, to have to pay that price. I do not want anyone who has been brave enough to break out of a painful situation to spend years spinning around, wondering what to do next.

## GILDED RETURNS

You may have picked up this book because you read *Gilded*. If so, welcome back! You are already familiar with this terrain. That book offered a way out of the gilded cage: the illusions of safety, status, and striving that masquerade as success while quietly hollowing us out. For many readers, myself included, naming the cage was the most liberating. Seeing it clearly was enough to initiate real change.

What *Gilded* could not answer—what *no first awakening* ever answers —is the harder, more sobering question: **What happens *after* you get out?**

It's one thing to experience insight. It's another to *live* from it. Anyone can have a breakthrough from a book, a seminar, or a moment of courage. However, living awake, day after day, without slipping back into old bargains is a different order of commitment entirely.

I confess, though I now clearly see the need for it (obviously), I didn't plan to write a sequel. I felt that *Gilded* was a complete work and assumed, like many authors and coaches, that if I ever wrote again, it would be on a new topic. Instead, this book was born of necessity. As *Gilded* was going to press, I began to notice a pattern I couldn't ignore. Highly-capable, deeply-reflective people—people fluent in the language of growth —were *still* stuck, but this time, not because they lacked tools or because they didn't understand the principles, but because they were unwilling to pay the actual cost of freedom. They knew how to leave the cage, in theory only. In practice, they refused to let go of what leaving would require.

One version of this looked like a woman who could speak eloquently about abundance, alignment, and wealth consciousness—someone who did every program, read every book, and traveled the world collecting insights and affirmations. On the surface, she embodied success. Underneath, she was quietly accumulating debt, postponing reality, and calling it "faith." When the numbers finally refused to cooperate, what emerged wasn't a fear of failure, but a refusal to face the deeper insecurities and self-betrayals that real abundance demands we confront.

Another version appeared as a man who arrived at a seminar in what he described as a "crisis of purpose." He left elated, inspired, and convinced he was ready to redesign his life. Months later, he gently admitted, almost apologetically, that he had changed nothing. When I asked the only question that mattered at that point—"*What are you still afraid of?*"—his answer was not professional uncertainty or lack of clarity. It was truth. He was living a life carefully constructed to avoid who he actually was and, in his case, his sexuality. Freedom, for him, would require dismantling the image that had kept him safe.

Again and again, I saw the same dynamic: people willing to do the work, as long as the work didn't cost them their identity, their image, or the approval they had organized their lives around. They wanted freedom without loss. Truth without disruption. Awakening without consequence. And that, I realized, is purgatory.

I had seen it before, of course. A brilliant woman forced into reinvention only after a devastating accident stripped away the scoreboard she had been clinging to. Another who understood every principle needed to live free yet chose suffering over the uncertainty of change; waiting, unconsciously, for life to force her hand.

There is no shame in this. But there is tragedy in waiting for catastrophe to grant permission to become yourself. Whether it's an Olympian who discovers that the medal is hollow until success becomes service, or a CEO who realizes the empire isn't enough without peace in their own skin, the truth is the same: **Freedom only becomes real when you are willing to stake your life on it.**

What these people, and I, eventually had to face is this: Insight is not transformation. Without the willingness to absorb the losses that truth demands—the collapse of facades, the discomfort of honesty, the relinquishing of identities that no longer fit—growth becomes performance. Awakening becomes rehearsal, and life, ultimately, remains unchanged.

I am not exempt from this pattern. Years after my own reckoning, after my return from Zurich and the rebuilding of my life, things began to go very well. My business grew quickly. Recognition followed. And quietly, almost imperceptibly, I found myself slipping back into old measures of worth: burning the candle at both ends, chasing validation, and mistaking visibility for value. Had I not been paying attention, had I not had the language and discipline to notice, I would have surely landed right back in the same purgatory I now recognize so clearly in others.

And that is why this book exists. *GILT FREE* is not an expansion of *Gilded*. It is a descent beneath it. If *Gilded* was about identifying what to release to break free, *GILT FREE* is about learning how to live once release has occurred—how to meet life as it actually is, with honesty when it's inconvenient, devotion when it's unglamorous, and resilience when success does or does not arrive.

## WHAT TO EXPECT

In the *Seinfeld* episode, "The Opposite," George Costanza realizes that every instinct he trusts leads him in the wrong direction. So, he tries something radical: He stops doing what feels right and does the opposite instead. Almost immediately, his life begins to improve. By the end of the episode, he proclaims, "Jerry, this is no longer a fleeting notion. This is my religion." It had set him free. The revelation isn't comedic—it's structural. What George stumbles onto is a principle I know to be 100% accurate: When the rules you're following keep producing the same failure, loyalty to them isn't discipline. It's a trap.

Using "The Opposite" framework from *Seinfeld* is what *GILT FREE* is built around. It's what I call *anti*-rules—small, counterintuitive actions that quietly undo the patterns keeping you stuck. Some may look deceptively simple like saying "no" without overexplaining, leaving a party early, sending the invoice without hesitation, or refusing to justify your existence. These moves are invisible to everyone else, but they hit at the core of the old programming, rewiring your nervous system, restoring your dignity, and opening the cage to freedom.

Here's what you can expect as you work your way through these *anti*-rules:

First, you may feel resistance. If so, that is good. Your resistance to this work (your feelings of being triggered), or even anger toward me or the text, is just the mask (your ego) trying to keep its job. Expect side effects such as bargaining ("Maybe later…"), righteousness ("I'm right, and she is SO wrong!"), and nostalgia ("It *used* to work, so why can't I just go back there?"). The persona is clever; it will pitch you a thousand familiar arguments. As you encounter them, I encourage you to write them down and to question them for their realness using the tools offered to you in the early chapters of this book. Then, as often as possible, make the opposite move and continue reading.

Second, you may feel grief. Individuation always costs you a fantasy—sometimes several. That if you behave, they will love you. That if you stay small and keep quiet, you'll be safe and get to stay (and, of course, that things will turn around for you without you having to break anything. Ha!). That if you never make waves, you will never drown. As these illusions shatter, you may begin to feel actual loss. If so, grieve the loss of the illusions and of the identity you constructed around them. They served you once, and you are allowed to be grateful for them, but, alas, they can't take you where you're going.

Third, you may feel spaciousness and reverence at many points throughout this work—a real sense of chill—which is likely unfamiliar to you. As you read passages that deeply resonate with you, the silence and peace that first felt like danger (or grief) may begin to feel wonderful. If so, go with it!

The more you can delve into and do this work, the more you will see new impulses and options appear: a bolder idea, a new client or job prospect, a different lover, a different routine. When this happens, know that the magnetism you are experiencing because of accepting peace is not magic—it's *mechanics*. When you stop reinforcing the old pattern, reality can return you to your factory settings: to be responsive, flexible, alive, and prosperous. Let me be blunt: Factory settings should feel good. You just worked so hard, you forgot that feeling. But as you progress through this book, that opposite—that OG—will come back to its rightful place.

Fourth, you may feel power. Not power-over (dominance), but power-within (inner strength). Authentic power. You will tap into the power that comes from peace, which arises from being congruent within yourself. You may feel the unshakable power that comes from saying what you mean and meaning what you say, from doing what you said you'd do, from declining what you can't carry, and from choosing your standards and then living inside them.

This is the pleasure Consuelo found in work that matched her conscience. This is the pleasure I found the day I decided that nothing I wore or achieved would ever again be permitted to explain me to myself, and that I would never betray myself by selling my soul for status and "security" ever again.

Since I've started this book with examples that include a duchess for the expansion of your possibilities and success, here is another exemplar you might consider for the journey ahead: you. Maybe you're reading this at a kitchen counter between your work-from-home meetings, or in a quiet room after a divorce, or waiting for your child to get done with soccer practice. You've done what you were supposed to do. You've built something that photographs well. Now, you want your *real life* to begin. This book contains answers where you need them, and support where you need it, too.

At various points in this book, we will get more specific than we did in *Gilded*. We'll talk about money, for example, because individuation without financial clarity is just a mood. We'll talk about relationships, because nothing exposes the mask like love, and nothing repairs it like truth. We'll talk about work, because work is where most high achievers hide their most brilliant form of self-abandonment, and because once you get *this* right, you will see that it can and will become one of your ultimate vessels for freedom, just like the first two. We'll talk about mastery and service without letting either become another audition. We will train your attention to stop scanning for external cues and start listening to internal ones. We will let go of outcomes that keep you in chains, identifying new moves that will ultimately compound into seismic shifts.

Before real change occurs, there's often a moment of disgust or exhaustion. Disgust with the secret you're still hiding, the debt you're still carrying, or the exhaustion from the hill you're still running up. Most people mistake these feelings for burnout or morph them into self-pity. Doing so would continue the self-betrayal and self-delusion. I see these as emotional signals of readiness. When you're finally sick of your own *Gilded* BS, that's the open doorway. That's when self-awareness becomes potent enough to act on. That's when *GILT FREE* can work.

Lest you fret that the opposite moves (*anti*-rules) I am about to present will look like the stuff of memes (*take the nap, send the invoice, ask for the raise, leave the party early, say "no" without an explanation*), let me assure you: The opposite moves will be invisible to everyone but you. Do not justify, do not underestimate yourself, do not rely on others so much, don't apologize for existing, don't edit your joy, don't borrow worry. The quiet, opposite moves are the ones that rewire your nervous system the fastest. They are the ones that counter cultural programming, that end anxiety and performance, and restore dignity at the molecular level. In fact, you will find that the *anti*-rules will help you get just about anything you want, including, and especially, joy by teaching you how to build a life where you don't need constant approval, to manipulate attention, and to check over your shoulder. You will see how fast this works. The results will speak for themselves.

## *GILT FREE*, NOT *GUILT* FREE

The title of this book, *GILT FREE*, warrants an important definition. **Guilt**—the real, internal alarm system, evolved to keep us in check—is not all bad. There is such a thing as healthy guilt. Healthy guilt is what tells you, "Stop. You're about to betray your values. You are about to *sell your soul.*" It's uncomfortable but necessary. Healthy guilt keeps you from building blind spots. It protects your future self.

**Gilt,** by contrast, is the shiny veneer of success. It's the appearance of winning at all costs. It's what happens when we train ourselves not to feel guilt. We build metrics and output instead of character; we prize optics over substance. And at scale, the system rewards that veneer, until it doesn't. You can get very far on Gilt, but you cannot stay whole.

This is why most dark-triad "winners" eventually implode or wind up miserable even if they keep their mansions. When your identity is tied to achievement without integrity, there's no internal compass left. The very emotion designed to keep you safe—*guilt*—is gone. And that is not freedom; that is self-destruction on delay.

*GILT FREE* is a handbook for reversing that. It is not about learning to out-Machiavelli the Machiavellians or to outmaneuver life. It's about refusing the blind spots, recovering your healthy guilt as a guide, and living without the shiny-but-hollow gilding. It's about becoming the rare person who succeeds and stays whole; someone who doesn't end up exiled from the village, in prison, or in a $43 million mansion tweeting at ghosts.

# Disclaimer

*"Before you heal someone, ask him if he's willing to give up
the things that make him sick."*
HIPPOCRATES

Not everyone will be ready for the radical honesty required in reading this book. Having coached thousands of people privately, I can tell you—with love and seriousness—many keep signing up for the next program, book, or coach believing they're moving forward, when, in fact, they're still in the cage. In doing so, they only deepen the pattern.

Another of Jung's famous quotes is "People will do anything, no matter how absurd, in order to avoid facing their own souls." Here again, he was right. I have watched people go to extreme, even illogical, lengths to avoid the uncomfortable task of truly liberating themselves and living as they are, including reading sequels to books that ask them to go inward and break free from lying before they have any intention of doing so. This is counter-productive but also logical: If your success has required you to become more ruthless than honest, this book will challenge you. Not because it is moralistic, but because it refuses to confuse power with goodness. If you are ready, then great! And if not, maybe give *Gilded* another go first?

*GILT FREE* is not merely about feeling better. It is about seeing clearly. About removing the polish of success that hides compromise, cruelty, and self-betrayal behind results.

# Shedding the Remaining Gilt

# Debunking the Great Folly

Most overachievers don't build their lives from desire or truth. They build from a quiet, relentless panic. The panic sounds like this:

*I need to get this right.*

*I can't fall behind.*

*If I lose this, I lose everything.*

*Once I fix this one thing, I'll finally be okay.*

*"I am not okay"* is rarely a conscious thought, but it is operative. It hums beneath ambition, fuels perfectionism, and disguises itself as responsibility, drive, and "high standards." It decides how hard you work, who you tolerate, what you chase, and what you are willing to sacrifice. It becomes the invisible architect of your life.

This is the reason so many successful, capable people end up exhausted, brittle, and quietly unhappy, even when everything "worked." In my first book, *Gilded,* I wrote about the illusion that hooks high achievers early: the belief that success will save us. That if we achieve enough, earn enough, or refine ourselves into something flawless, we will finally feel worthy, safe, and whole. But illusions don't disappear just because we see through them once.

Going back to my own Gilded-cage story: Many years before this business took off and the second phase of my life took off, as you may recall—I lived in a proper Gilded Cage—a well-furnished, chic apartment in Zurich. I had a marriage that looked good on paper. A career that impressed strangers. From the outside, it was a golden life. On the inside, I was suffocating. If you had audited any single area of my life then, you would have found evidence of "success." What you would not have seen were the thoughts running the show:

*If I work hard enough, I'll be safe.*

*If I look perfect enough, I'll be loved.*

*If I succeed enough, I'll be okay.*

Every choice I made—every overextension, every compromise, every silence—rested on the same poisonous premise: I was not already okay. It primed me for the Cage.

Most of us pick up this belief early. For me, it crystallized in adolescence, right around the moment I learned how much popularity, performance, and approval mattered. From that point on, my life became a frantic attempt to close an imaginary gap between *not okay* and *okay*. That gap is where suffering lives. Before we can build anything real, before we can live free, we have to flatten the ground it stands on.

## LAYING THE MENTAL FOUNDATION FOR YOUR HIGHER SELF

Maybe high school is when the dark premise that you are *not okay* took hold of you, too. No matter when you picked it up, as you may recall from *Gilded*, that premise is the foundation of the Scarcity Mindset that dominates most of our lives; the one we can, unfortunately, slip back into. If you are reading this because your results are still not pleasing to you, and you are not yet living your dream life and/or dream mental state, then it's important to reach back and call it out so you can flatten the surface. Again.

Scarcity is the great lie of our time. It is the illusion that there is not enough: not enough time, not enough money, not enough success, or not enough love. And if there is not enough, then *I* am not enough. And if I am not enough, I am *not* okay.

This scarcity mindset is whispered into our ears from our earliest days by well-meaning people, like our parents, teachers, and pretty much everyone else. It shapes how we see ourselves and what we settle for. It convinces us that the cage is safety, that striving is salvation (you must never, ever take a break), that exhaustion is noble. But scarcity can only ever produce more scarcity. It is an endless loop of "not enough." A relentless, perfectionistic, ambitious pursuit of more.

The truth, which I could not see back in high school, is that abundance (the opposite of scarcity in all its forms, like goodness, love, joy, personal fulfillment) is not something to be earned. Abundance is reality, and the abundance mindset is the reality that there is more than enough. It is what is always here when the lie of scarcity dissolves. When the temporary lie known as "the dark" dissolves, that's the moment light is no longer obstructed. It is the knowing that you are, already and always, *okay*.

## MUCH ADO ABOUT ABUNDANCE

All you need to do to break past the scarcity mindset is learn to challenge it, again and again. Start by recognizing scarcity thoughts, then actively challenge the thoughts. Are they true? This will help reframe negatives into positives, help you be more willing to try alternatives, reorient yourself toward focusing on growth and learning, and eventually shift your focus to abundance.

And yeah, we do *have* to keep doing this. In all my years of coaching, I have only met two people who sincerely seemed to have made a permanent switch to abundance in all facets of their life. What are the odds you are like them and not like the rest of us?

## BETTER CONCRETE

Once the ground is cleared, the next decision matters more than most people realize: deciding what you pour into the foundation. As it turns out, not all concrete is created equal. Some mixtures look solid at first but fracture under pressure. They crack when temperatures change. They crumble when weight is added. They require constant patching and reinforcement, and even then, they never quite hold.

Most people build their lives on exactly this kind of inferior material.

*They anchor themselves to **popularity**.*

*They brace their choices against **FOMO**.*

*They let **obligation** harden into law.*

These *feel* sturdy because they are socially reinforced. Everyone uses them. Everyone enforces them. Alas, as I am sure you have noticed by now, they are structurally unsound. They cannot support freedom. They cannot withstand change. And they will keep you in quiet captivity for as long as you rely on them.

**Popularity** makes you perform.

**FOMO** makes you chase.

**Obligation** makes you comply.

Together, they form a foundation that keeps you exquisitely managed by other people's expectations, timelines, moods, and approval. So, this is the upgrade point. If you are going to build a life that does not crack under scrutiny, pressure, or success itself, you must be ruthless about the materials you allow into the base. That means identifying the substances that once kept you accepted, but now keep you small, and refusing to pour them again.

We are not reinforcing the old structure. We are replacing it. Beginning with popularity and ending with obligation.

## POPULARITY

Popularity is perhaps the most deceptive of the three old materials that nip at the heels of any overachiever. At its core, it's the hope that if enough people approve of you, you'll finally feel secure. It demands constant performance, a rounding of your edges, a dilution of your originality, and a lot of "likes." To be popular is to spend your life auditioning; trying to please the faceless crowd rather than listening to your own voice.

Of course, popularity is fickle because people are fickle. To build anything upon it is to build on quicksand, as the masses will crown you one day and cancel you the next. If you anchor your worth to being liked, you will forever be contorting. You will never risk the boldness required for true creativity, leadership, or intimacy.

## FOMO

If popularity is the need to be seen, FOMO (fear of missing out) is the need to be *everywhere*. It whispers that life is happening out there, at that dinner, that trip, that launch party—without you. You run from one to another, chasing other people's timelines, saying "yes" when you mean "no," scrolling feeds until your eyes sting, convinced that fulfillment lies just beyond your grasp.

FOMO, of course, is another lie. The life you're afraid of missing is already here. It exists in your body, your breath, this moment. Each time you bow to FOMO, you abandon yourself and your own agenda.

## OBLIGATION

And then there is obligation, the most gilded material of all. With more success of the gilded kind—bigger careers, bigger houses, bigger reputations—comes a heavier yoke of "shoulds." You become a prisoner of roles, marriages, standards, and rules that don't even belong to you. Your calendar fills with commitments that keep you busy but not alive.

Obligation robs you of choice. It keeps you stuck in a life that looks good on the outside but feels hollow on the inside.

The good news? It's possible to break out of each of these. The bad news is that it's way easier said than done. (Which you may have already realized since you are reading a sequel.) You are in the *in-between*: be-tween breaking out of the gilded cage and manifesting your free life. The in-between is not comfortable.

Emotional discomfort—the discomfort that comes with radical hon-esty—is the price of admission to your new level. It is the portal. As you drop the need to be liked for long enough to tell the truth, to be every-where, and to appease everyone, you will feel the tremors. Others may accuse you of being selfish. You may disappoint, disagree, or disconnect.

My advice? Plow through. Getting a plane off the ground, I am told, is usually the trickiest bit of the journey.

## WHAT HAPPENS ON THE WAY UP: THE LIFE YOU BUILT COLLAPSES… TWICE

Author Jen Hatmaker knows what happens when you begin to collapse your obligation-serving identity (the former perfectionist, populari-ty-seeking, overachiever self) at the onset of an inner journey. In fact, on her way out of her own gilded cage, she found out what happens—twice.

For those of you who don't know what comes next and are unfamiliar with her story, here it is. Jen, like many of us, also built her entire life on being "good." From the very young age of 19, she was a model evangelical wife, mother, and Christian influencer; the darling of her community. She was funny, relatable, and shiny enough to inspire envy, but never so shiny as to threaten the story. Her marriage, her church, her career, her very identity were all woven from that same fabric.

For years, it worked. She pulled off the charade. The first rupture in her perfect pink bubble came when she began to speak her truth. Jen could no longer reconcile what she believed about love and justice with the doc-trines she had been taught, so she began to voice support for LGBTQ+ rights. It was as though the trapdoor beneath her life swung open. Suddenly, her books were pulled from shelves, her publisher distanced itself from her, and invitations disappeared overnight. She was recast from darling to pariah.

Then came the second collapse. In 2020, Jen discovered that her husband of twenty-six years was unfaithful. While betrayal was shocking enough, the divorce that followed was devastating. In one season, she lost both institutions that had once held her life together: marriage and church. And she had to face the terrifying question so many of us eventually have to answer: *If I am no longer who I thought I was—the wife, the influencer, the golden girl of a system—then who am I?* And also: *What if I never was that golden girl, but just… gilded?*

Jen's answers were not immediate, and they were not clean. (They rarely are.) At first, she grieved, she raged. After all, she had been shamed, humiliated, scapegoated, and even gaslit—told by loved ones that her suffering was divine punishment for walking away from the roles she was supposed to play. Slowly, piece by piece, she began to rebuild the only temple that mattered: her sense of self. As she grew, Jen began to write again, this time more honestly. She examined her complicity, her patterns, her codependency, and began to experience, for the very first time in her life, what it meant to live independently, as her own person, with her own worth intact. Today, she is doing just that. Not perfect, but becoming free, and totally cool with life as it is.

Jen's story illustrates the very heart of this book. We are conditioned to believe that safety lies in the cage: in roles, in identities, in fulfilling our obligations, in getting other people's approval and systems that promise belonging if we contort ourselves small enough to fit. But when those cages inevitably crack through disillusionment, betrayal, or collapse, we are forced into a reckoning. In that reckoning—with scarcity, with popularity, with FOMO, and with obligation—we will meet our *true* worldview. And we will have a chance to overwrite it.

## THE ENLIGHTENMENT DETOUR: YOUR NEW LIFE WILL COST YOU YOUR OLD ONE

*"The truth will set you free, but first it will piss you off."*
GLORIA STEINEM

When Consuelo Vanderbilt told her mother she was leaving her husband, she wasn't just ending a marriage. She was detonating an entire worldview. That union had been engineered as a social triumph: status secured, appearances preserved, legitimacy earned. For Consuelo to walk away wasn't merely inconvenient. It was treason. A refusal to continue playing her assigned role.

This is the part no one warns you about when you begin to wake up.

Rattling the cage doesn't just scare you. It threatens the people who benefit from you staying inside it. When you stop operating from the premise that *I am not okay* and begin, tentatively at first, to presume that you are, something irreversible happens. Your decisions change. You stop saying "yes" automatically. You stop chasing approval. You stop treating FOMO, popularity, and obligation as legitimate authorities. Almost immediately, your environment pushes back.

"You've changed," they say, not as praise, but as accusation. Not because you're wrong, but because your freedom disrupts contracts you never realized you signed. It exposes illusions others are still invested in maintaining. This phase is uncomfortable not just internally but relationally. This is what I call the Enlightenment Detour. It isn't glamorous. It isn't tidy. And it costs you something real: the version of your life that depended on you staying agreeable, compliant, and quietly unfree.

When people begin to wake up, whether it be through therapy, coaching, burnout, grief, a breakup, or a midlife crisis, I see the same pattern again and again. They pull away from the world temporarily so they can internalize what they're learning. Not because they're arrogant, but because if they don't create space, they won't be allowed to change at all.

At first, the inner journey feels like pure light. Cosmic *aha* moments. Relief. Clarity. You realize the life you've been living isn't working, and the rules you inherited were never really yours. Then comes the harder realization: The people who shaped you, lovable though they may be, are human and, therefore, flawed. It's exhilarating and heartbreaking all at once.

Often, that clarity triggers an overcorrection. Instead of integration, we go reactive. We lash out. This impulse is developmentally familiar. It's the same instinct teenagers act out during adolescence when individuation requires pushing against authority. Translation: Announce how awake we are and how asleep everyone else is. We cut cords. We go "low contact." We install fortress-level boundaries. We mute the group chat. We unfollow our cousins.

Once more: *This is the detour.*

For a while, it has to be this way. You are pulling yourself out of the gravitational field of your conditioning. The mistake is not entering the detour. The mistake is believing it's the destination.

It isn't.

The detour was not the end point for me, for Jen Hatmaker, or for Consuelo Vanderbilt, and it will not be for you either. Eventually, if you keep going, something shifts. You realize healing was never meant to build walls. It cannot exist inside them. Healing builds bridges, bridges that allow you to love people without agreeing with them, to have boundaries without contempt, to stand in your truth without needing outrage to prop up your worth.

If you're in the detour right now—mad, sad, and drafting long messages to your mother that you will later delete—I see you. I've been there. It's brutal while you're in it. But this much I know: The work does not end in isolation. Freedom of thought does not require loneliness. And true enlightenment does not ask you to burn everything behind you; only the illusions that kept you from yourself.

Consider, if you are in it right now, that many people never get here at all. Not because they lack insight, but because they are unwilling to disappoint anyone along the way. They do the reading and understand the language, but when growth requires them to unsettle a relationship, challenge an expectation, or be misunderstood, they stop. You are being brave here.

*Keep going.*


## NO MORE FAUSTIAN BARGAINS

There's an episode of *Frasier* called "The Devil and Dr. Phil" in which Frasier Crane discovers that his old colleague, the far more famous Dr. Phil, is represented by Frasier's own agent, the ruthlessly amoral Bebe Glazer. Bebe, knowing Frasier's weakness for prestige, offers to represent him again, after the two had broken up over her lack of scruples. Frasier opts to forget their past moral incompatibility and agrees to strike a deal. Fame, at last, is within reach.

When Frasier tells his brother Niles about the deal he's about to make, Niles grows uneasy. The whole thing sounds suspiciously Faustian, he warns. Frasier pauses, then replies with one of the funniest lines in the series, *"Faust was a moron."*

That line lands, because it exposes a truth most of us don't want to admit: We all believe *we* would make the deal more intelligently. Cleaner. With better boundaries. We assume we'll take the upside without paying the price.

But gilded living is, in essence, a Faustian bargain.

Faust is the original cautionary tale. In the old legend, Dr. Faust trades his soul to the devil in exchange for knowledge, power, and worldly pleasure. It's the first and most famous example of a deal that looks brilliant in the moment and ruins you in the end. A Faustian bargain, then, is not simply a bad deal. It's a specific kind of deal; one where you trade something essential—your integrity, your truth, your freedom—for something that promises safety, status, or belonging. It feels like relief. It looks like winning. It's like marrying for money—it always comes with a hidden cost. You get what you asked for and slowly lose yourself in the process.

Every time we uphold a lie to belong, to survive, or to maintain proximity to power, we make a Faustian deal. We preserve the image and sacrifice the self. We choose belonging in the gilded room over belonging to ourselves.

The good news is, the bargain dissolves the moment you stop making it, which is the very moment you refuse to sell your soul and your authenticity for acceptance, for money, or for status by *walking away*. When you can do that, simply by stating the truth and acting with integrity at any cost, you have already stepped out of the cage.

While you may be terrified for your future in the metaphorical cabinet that kept you safe, or so you thought, you will soon realize that only now, after expressing yourself truly, you are finally free.

## AFTER FAUST: THE OBLIGATION IS TO YOURSELF

The quiet cost of obligation and popularity-seeking is having to lie politely, socially, and constantly. Over time, lying of any kind doesn't just erode relationships, it erodes the relationship with yourself. Telling the truth, then, is not merely about being candid with others. It inevitably entails asking for what you need, too. This is where many people get stuck because they've been taught that naming needs is selfish, demanding, or socially dangerous.

It isn't. It is self-compassion in action.

As Dr. Kristin Neff, author of *Self-Compassion*, writes: *"When we truly care for ourselves, we're better able to care for others."* This is not because we become nicer, but because we stop resenting those whom we've been over-accommodating. When you begin asking the question *"What do I need?"* something profound happens. That question becomes a compass, quietly orienting you back toward alignment. Toward your values. These values are not what you admire or post about; they are the things you *refuse to betray*. These are and should be your deepest commitments, to yourself first, and then to others.

This is why telling the truth and naming your needs are new skills you will need as you begin your journey to self-belonging. Telling the truth and being honest about who you are and what you want are the foundation of sustainable leadership and healthy relationships. They prevent resentment from accumulating. They interrupt self-abandonment. And they give others a clear, trustworthy signal about who you are, and how to be with you.

So before your next big decision, your next difficult conversation, or your next reflexive yes, pause and ask yourself:

*What do I need to do right now to stay in integrity?*

Then, act on the answer, even if it feels awkward. Even if it costs you approval.

# REFLECTION
# BUSTING THE FAUSTIAN FOLLY

Journal on the questions below.

1.  **What is the silent bargain I've been making with *myself*?**
    (For example: *If I achieve X, then I'll finally feel okay. If I keep X at bay, then I will obtain Y.*)

2.  **Where in my life is that bargain still active? Where do I still confuse "safety" with the cage?**
    (A role, an identity, a relationship, a belief?)

3.  **When did I first learn that I was "not enough?"**
    How has that story been running my life since?

4.  **If I already knew—right now—that I am okay, that abundance is real, how would my choices shift today?**

Review your answers. When you notice the bargains, they begin to dissolve.

# Make a Statement

*"At the moment of commitment, the Universe conspires to assist you."*
JOHANN WOLFGANG VON GOETHE

As we have established here from the get go, most high achievers don't fail to change their lives because they lack insight; they fail because they stop just short of following through with action.

They *see* the patterns. Most, I have found, can name the wounds, the conditioning, and the traps. But then they still wait for clarity, for confidence, for permission, or for the moment when change will feel less disruptive. That moment will never come, nor land, because clarity without movement doesn't hold. Awareness alone does not re-root a life.

There comes a moment in every real transformation when being on "Team Gets It" is no longer enough. You'll feel it, because it will be the point at which staying the same (upholding the Faustian bargain, maintaining the appearances, continuing to struggle with the same issues, over and over) becomes far more uncomfortable than the risk of changing. When the work stops being internal and starts asking something visible of you, you will know it because that moment is not subtle and it is not symbolic.

So, stop meeting it with symbolic subtleties. Instead, *make a statement*. A statement is not an intention. It's not an announcement. It's not a perfectly-articulated plan. A statement is an action, often a risky one, that is so aligned with your emerging truth that your environment has to respond.

Think of it as choosing your flooring for a new home. You are anchoring the ground upon which your new identity will stand. This is the difference between deciding you want a different life and beginning to live like you mean it. It's the moment you "put a ring" on your future and say, *I'm in.*

When I finally made my own statement, it didn't look dramatic from the outside. But it felt radical to me. All I did was move back to New York City, and this time *not* to the life I already knew. I chose a new neighborhood: the Upper East Side (for those reading now who are non-New Yorkers, you should know that the Upper East Side *is* considered chic but is *not* considered cool). In doing so, I defied the FOMO and ditched popularity at the door by leaving behind the familiarity of downtown bars, late-night brunches, and every performative, chaotic obligation of my former cool, single life. I traded my edgy, ironic, Prada-clad, perpetually-exhausted social circle for—gasp—married, uptown friends with routines, boundaries, and… different taste.

I also moved into an apartment that was wildly outside my budget, because I insisted on living directly in Central Park, in a space that was genuinely beautiful and that I adored. This was my statement.

*A financial risk.*

*A social risk.*

*A declaration.*

For the first time, I chose something fully on behalf of the life I wanted. Not based on FOMO, not based on what I could "justify," and not based on outside pressure. I started to live like I meant it.

Slowly, something remarkable happened. All those uptown places I had dismissed for years? They were better. In every way. Calmer. Kinder. More spacious. More thoughtfully designed. They offered stability, grace, and a kind of quiet wealth—both financial and spiritual—that I had never known before. With a mild sense of shock, I realized: *This feels far more like me.*

Occasionally, I'd run into friends from my former life, still circling the same parties, the same situationships, the same ghost-of-*Sex-and-the-City* fantasy, and I'd feel a brief pang of shame, followed by something softer and more honest: compassion. I'd think, sincerely, *What were we thinking?*

This isn't a mean thought. It's a sobering one. It's the moment you realize the illusion is over. The emperor never had any clothes. Once you see that, your next moves become easier, because you will learn what it feels like—what the truth feels like. After you learn how the truth feels, your nervous system starts rejecting what no longer fits, what is *not* in integrity. The longer you immerse yourself in better environments, the more they shape you. Over time, you don't just live somewhere new.

You become someone new.

Just ask Julia Child.

When she first arrived in France, she was awkward, uncertain, and completely out of her depth. She was an American housewife fumbling through an unfamiliar language, and unfamiliar markets and customs. But immersion changes people. Through food, culture, rhythm, and devotion to craft, Julia didn't just learn to cook. She became alive. Expressive. Passionate. Unapologetically herself.

She didn't just live in Paris. She became Parisian in the only way that matters—speaking French, eating French, befriending the French, and leaving California (her home state) far behind. This is how transformation actually happens. To move beyond fear and FOMO and into a higher-vibration life, you must make such a statement; one bold move that places you *inside* a reality that reflects who you are becoming, not who you've been rehearsing.

That statement might look like a new neighborhood, a new city, or a new home. It might look like a new relationship, or the courageous ending of one that no longer fits. It may be learning a new skill, starting a business, or radically reworking how you spend your time. Sometimes it's as simple—and as radical—as saying no to busywork and yes to rest, pleasure, and spaciousness.

But in the realm of statement-making, there is one move more powerful than almost any other: changing your company. Who you spend time with, take cues from, and give access to your energy. Very often, the boldest statement you make isn't about geography or career at all. It's allowing your inner change to be reflected outwardly, even when that disappoints others. Which brings us back, inevitably, to the Enlightenment Detour.

## A SOBERING EXERCISE

Take a moment and write down the five people you spend the most time with. Once you have their names, rank them—emotionally, financially, energetically—from 1 to 10, where 1 feels depleted or stagnant and 10 feels like a living role model. If your life feels stuck, flat, or strangely dissatisfying, you will almost always see the mirror here. This list is your current frame of reference. It may not delight you.

The good news? It makes your statement move fairly obvious, even if it won't make it easier. If your company is not who you wish to become, or does not match where you want to go, you will have to expand or replace that immediate circle.

When you level up your company, your life follows. In fact, it often works in reverse: When you deliberately place yourself among more-elevated people, you rise to meet them. This isn't magic, it's proximity. It's mirror neurons. It's biology and psychology doing what they do best.

We all resist change, because the familiar feels safe, even when it isn't. That's why we play not to lose instead of playing to win—as I did, staying in a horrid relationship for four years, or playing small in my career for so long. Doing the opposite—making bold moves, going for the promotion, finding aligned company—requires stepping out of the familiar entirely and choosing something new.

Aside from changing where you live, one of the most effective ways to do this is to consciously curate your company. Seek out people who are joyful, generous, emotionally stable, honest, healthy, and prosperous in ways that are not performative. People who are creating their lives rather than reacting to them.

In case you have not gotten the message yet—this may mean getting new friends.

Important note: To get new friends, you *don't* need to abandon anyone or announce your awakening. But if you are surrounded by chronic complainers, chaos addicts, or people who are fundamentally disengaged from their own growth, it will be almost impossible to move forward without being pulled back.

This is why I recommend high-level communities and masterminds, whether that's my advanced coaching cohort, *The Club*, or any environment where people are committed to living with integrity, responsibility, and excellence. I have seen, repeatedly, what happens when people immerse themselves in a different crowd: They recalibrate what "normal" looks like. And then their lives reorganize around that new normal.

When I moved into that Upper East Side townhouse, with Central Park practically brushing my doorstep, I wasn't just upgrading my zip code. I was upgrading my new normal and, with it, my self-concept. I was marinating in a new identity. I couldn't afford the place, at least not on paper. My application was thin, the realtor knew it, and yet I knew, with total clarity: This is where my next chapter begins.

So, I did what any woman on a mission would do. I stalked the realtor at her synagogue (shout-out to Temple Emanu-El), showed up in my best Shabbat attire with a chocolate babka, "accidentally" bumped into her, and followed up with a handwritten letter—and a note from my rabbi attesting to my good character.

It worked.

That apartment became my sanctuary. A sacred space. A stake in the ground. It represented a choice to stop waiting to feel ready and start living like I already was. This is what statement moves do. They stabilize identity. They make it harder to slide backward into old patterns of perfectionism, social climbing, and applause-seeking.

The statement move is imperative; *not* making it is why people so often get stuck after coaching programs or life-changing books. They gain insight, but they *don't* change their surroundings. Or they make one move, then retreat back into familiar environments that quietly reinforce the old self. No move, no move on up.

Transformation requires motion. And then, crucially, returning to the inner work again, from a new place. As Julia Child became Parisian, as Consuelo became free, as I became myself in that sunlit townhouse, so, too, will you—*in motion*—become more and more of who you truly are.

# REFLECTION EXERCISE
# WHO ARE YOU BECOMING?

Take 10 minutes and journal your answers.

1.  **Environment:** Where are you still spending time that belongs to your *former* self? Which spaces (physical or digital) no longer reflect who you're becoming?

2.  **People:** Who in your current circle lights you up? Who drains you? What would it look like to deliberately spend more time with those who light you up?

3.  **Identity:** What's one "Upper East Side move" you know you're ready for—a symbolic step that would stretch you into your next self-concept?

4.  **Fear vs. Faith:** Where are you still "playing not to lose?" What's one opposite move you could make this week that would be playing to win?

5.  **Integration:** Imagine yourself five years from now, fully gilt free. What environments surround you? Who are the people at your table? How does it feel to live there?

6.  Based on the above answers: What is one big, undeniable action you are willing to take to "put a ring on" your decision?

# Stretching to New Limits

*"To continue to grow and learn, you must be willing to update, expand, and edit your identity. In many ways, growth is unlearning."*
JAMES CLEAR

There is a moment after any real change when life grows strangely quiet. You've made the move. You've shifted the environment. You've said "no" where you once said "yes." You are keeping some better, more supportive, and more inspiring company. On the outside, things look better: You are calmer, your surroundings are cleaner, and work feels more organic. And yet, something subtle begins to happen inside you. Old instincts start knocking. Familiar doubts creep back in. You find yourself reaching, unconsciously, for the very patterns you thought you'd left behind.

This is not failure. It's *biology*.

Research shows that human beings are governed by internal "set points," or unconscious identity thresholds, that determine what feels safe, normal, and deserved. When life improves faster than identity expands, the nervous system interprets it as a threat. And so, quietly, we self-correct. We sabotage or shrink, and a lot of us go running back to what we know. This is why so many people change their circumstances, only to recreate the same life in a new setting.

What you are or might be feeling now—the tension, the stretch, the urge to retreat—is not a sign that the move was wrong. It's a sign that your identity hasn't caught up yet. What needs to happen now is an internal recalibration of your inner GPS system, calculating a new route, to a new definition of success. If you do not define what "it all" looks like, your old inner GPS will just keep going back to the same spot.

## THE OLD "ALL"

The old version of success is a cultural inheritance. We absorb it without consent:

- Get the degree.
- Climb the ranks.
- Earn more money.
- Acquire more status.
- Collect external proof that you matter.

This definition of success is linear, narrow, and comparative. It's built on surrogate markers: titles, trophies, things you can show off. Author Jim Collins calls these "false proxies." I call it *the gilded cage*. Here's what each has in common: The old "all" as a goal post is always just out of reach, because it is, well, *false*. The moment you arrive at the corner office, someone else is already in the bigger office upstairs. The second your book hits the best-seller list, another book dethrones it.

The chase never ends. Purgatory sounds like a continuous loop of *"recalculating route."*

## THE NEW "ALL"

The new definition of success isn't external, it's internal. It's not about *having more*, it's about *being more*. At its core, redefining success means aiming for the ultimate destinations, including self-actualization—the freedom to live from your true self (which is, as Maslow defined it, "when you *must* be all that you *can* be")—and unity, the experience of belonging and creating beyond ego.

When you redefine success, "having it all" means:

- **Alignment**—living in integrity with your values, which has the effect of producing an inner good mood or inner clarity.
- **Authenticity**—dropping the performance and letting yourself be real.
- **Aliveness (mastery)**—choosing joy, play, and wonder, not just productivity.
- **Impact**—measuring your work by the lives you touch, not the likes you get.
- **Peace**—valuing your inner state as much as your outer accomplishments.

Swap these for the old MO, and you will soon be hearing the GPS say, "*You have arrived at your destination.*"

## ALIGNMENT IS THE NEW BLACK

What it takes to move further into your new identity is to now go beyond pouring the new concrete beneath your feet (choosing abundance) and selecting your new floor (making a bold move from abundance) by calibrating your thoughts, decisions, and moves not with your external circumstances but with inner *alignment*. Alignment is an unshakable, calm inner state, a good mood, or a feeling of clarity. It's born of freedom from the old scoreboard and from any other external or arbitrary standards and obligations. This is what many call authenticity, a freedom from posturing or from persona. Others call this inner peace, which is a feeling of unity within yourself and with the world.

Alignment, the new mode of having it "all," *isn't* less ambitious or materially empty. In fact, it's way braver, because it asks you to live on your own terms, and it usually makes you far richer, too. Just like the old American Express tagline went, *"Don't leave home without it."* Seriously, do not make decisions without alignment. Do not approach a conflict or negotiation without it and do not ask for what you want before you emotionally link up with it, because, again, the alignment *is* what you want.

Here's the caveat: You must be willing to go there. You must choose the new definition for having it all, and you will need to walk the walk of alignment. As we have established, to redefine success, you have to:

- Walk away from old scoreboards and, as such, let down your society.

- Drop your impossible standards (don't worry, you will not drop the high standards, just the impossible ones).
- Disappoint people who benefited from your over-functioning.
- Face the fear that if you stop proving yourself, you'll disappear.

This is the leap Gay Hendricks calls crossing the "Upper Limit" in his masterful book, *The Big Leap*. It's the "surrender" Michael Singer describes in *The Surrender Experiment*: the choice of letting go of what the world told you to cling to. It's Jung's individuation concept—the act of choosing wholeness over persona.

The willingness isn't theoretical. It's a daily reality. Every time you pause, ask yourself:

- *Is this choice mine or someone else's?*
- *Am I just chasing **more** or really choosing better?*
- *What would "all" look like if it was rooted in peace, purpose, and play?*

## THE PROMISE OF REDEFINITION

In 2020, like many of you, I ran out of shows to watch on Netflix and happened upon the absolute last resort: a sports documentary called *The Last Dance*. My interest in sports had, until this point, been negligible, to say the least, but as each of the series' many, many hours unfolded, I found myself more riveted and more and more in love. This was the story of rising from a group of superstars disjointed and egoic into a team united—all because they discovered a new idea of success. It is the story of the 1990s Chicago Bulls.

At first, Michael Jordan, a superstar if there ever was one, dominated as a key player and wanted glory for himself—which was reinforced by then coach Doug Collins. He wanted the title, the MVPs, the scoring records, and with Doug, he got them, but they never translated to wins for the team.

Not until a new coach, Phil Jackson, intervened. Phil harbored hopes for the team's glory and for long-term success. That's when Jordan redefined his own notion of success from *glory for me* to *glory for all of us* and the dynasty truly began. Under Coach Jackson's masterful tutelage and incessant insistence on something called "the triangle offense," Jordan stopped being just the most dazzling player on the court and started becoming the kind of leader who lifted every single man on that roster. It appears that almost everyone else learned that lesson throughout the series, too.

That shift from *me, me, me* to *we*, from striving for the spotlight to building a system that everyone could shine in, is what turned a once-exhausted star into the anchor of the greatest team of all time. In 1989, the Chicago Bulls had no championships. They had talent, and they had Jordan, but they also had frustration and burnout. By 1998, they had six rings and an unshakable culture that every franchise in every sport still studies today—*how is that for a stretch?*

That shift resulted in something bigger than basketball superstardom.

It marked a move from raw freedom—Jordan playing as he pleased under Coach Doug—to alignment and unity, where each player's greatness amplified the others. That's the secret: Freedom without unity still isolates, and unity without freedom still suffocates. Real success is *both*, in balance.

Maybe this is a metaphor, again, for your trajectory. Until now, you swam alone, enjoying temporary wins at best, and highs have not lasted (I mean, be honest, how's that working for you?). If this is not enough for you anymore, then what you stand to gain is the strength of the 1998 Bulls: a victory that comes with friendships, unity, and legacy.

This is the journey we're about to take: from chasing to choosing, from fractured to whole, from the *gilded* illusion of success to the gold standard of it. From the 1989 Chicago Bulls to the *1998, Greatest of All Time Chicago Friggin' Bulls.*

When you redefine success (especially when introducing the idea of freedom as *freedom from obligation*), this is what happens. You stop living in comparison and start living in creation. You stop hustling to earn rest and begin creating *from* rest. You stop measuring your worth in numbers and start feeling it in your bones. You win, bigly.

That's when you realize you really can have it all; not the old "all," not the exhausting all, but *the new-free, collaborative, supercharged all.* Redefining success, you will see, isn't just freedom from the gilded cage; it's your declaration of unity with yourself, your purpose, and with the people you're here to serve.

This is a true identity-level upgrade and once you make that upgrade, everything becomes possible for you. And it comes to you with far greater ease.

# REFLECTION
# CHOOSING A NEW KIND OF SUCCESS

Take 10 minutes and journal your answers.

1.  What's your current definition of "all?" Make a list.

2.  Circle anything on the list that makes up "it all" but is a proxy, something you think will *prove* you're enough.

3.  What on your list is just stuff you have to do and/or maintain for the approval of others?

4.  If you stripped away the proxies, what would your *true* "all" look like?

5.  What are you willing to let go of, today, to begin living into this new definition?

If you have answered these questions honestly and are satisfied, then the de-gilding section is, for now, complete.

# PART II

# Living GOLD

Most of my clients are, by all reasonable accounts, clever and accomplished persons possessed of a comfortable home, a functional life, and a disposition that has carried them without scandal or catastrophe precisely to where they now stand—at the top of their respective fields. These circumstances might be said to "unite many of the best blessings of existence." That's how "Jane Austen" they each sounded to me when we first met.

And yet, here they are, with me, preparing to interfere with them. Not with drama, nor with rebellion, nor with any great public undoing, but with something far more destabilizing in polite society: the decision to go all in on *their* life, on *their* terms.

This moment calls to mind that scene from *Seinfeld* that perfectly captures the decision I'm describing—that scene, from which, as I mentioned, we're about to borrow a philosophical framework for this book. George Costanza walks into the café where the gang always gathers, and looking particularly sullen, asks the question that lands as comedy only because it is so uncomfortably sincere: "How did it all go wrong for me? I had so much promise."

The joke, of course, is exaggeration. The insight is more serious. George's real problem is not that his life went wrong, but that his instincts—however confident—have been consistently unreliable guides. I see this all the time. It's not that they say these exact words, but… I hear them.

Part I of this book was about recognizing the problem in yourself.

It was about removal. It was about naming the illusions that kept you striving long after striving stopped serving you. It was about identifying the subtle forms of gilt that linger even after the obvious cage door swings open, the reflex to prove, the inherited obligations, the perfectionistic conditioning that insists your worth must still be earned, justified, or displayed.

Together, we stripped those layers back. We flattened the surface. We widened your definition of success, introduced an abundance mindset that is not aspirational but structural, and we cleared the terrain where an old identity once stood. That work matters more than most people realize, because without it, everything that comes next collapses. You cannot build a free life on a warped foundation. You cannot pour new meaning onto cracked ground. So, if you feel, at this juncture, a quiet sense of exposure—less armored, less performative, more spacious—that is not a problem. It is evidence that the demolition worked.

But here is the part no one tells you: Freedom does not arrive fully furnished.

Leaving the gilded cage only finishes answering, or revisits, that first question: *What am I no longer willing to live inside?* It does not yet answer the more practical one at the heart of this book: *How do I live now?* How do you choose, decide, commit, relate, and work when you are no longer driven by fear, by proving, or by survival-level ambition?

Part II is about answering that question directly, concretely, and without spiritual bypassing. It is about embodiment. It's about installing a way of living that does not depend on pressure to function, motivation to matter, or exhaustion as proof of worth. Not in theory but in practice. This is where we stop talking about detoxing ambition and start talking about construction.

The framework that follows is what I call **GOLD**:
> **G—Good Enough**
> **O—Open**
> **L—Lit Up**
> **D—Devoted**

These are not traits. They are commitments—daily orientations that replace the old operating system with one that can sustain freedom. It's enoughness that raises the floor beneath your life. Openness that ends the illusion of control. Aliveness that reconnects you to desire without addiction. Devotion that anchors your energy to something larger than recognition without dragging you back into obligation.

To walk the walk and live gilt free, you *need* these. You need a container; a reliable inner framework to make decisions once the pressure is gone. Not motivation. Not mood. Not willpower. A structure. Think of it as upgrading from a leaky bucket to a sturdy vessel—one that can hold your newfound sense of worth.

As Brené Brown writes in *Dare to Lead*, leadership—of others, and first of your own life—requires an inner container; a steady internal structure that helps you stay grounded, truthful, and discerning amid uncertainty. With it, you stop leaking energy. You stop outsourcing authority. You stop reacting and start choosing.

For me, this inner container is a *thinking system*. A thinking system is not a mindset or a set of beliefs you repeat to yourself. It is the invisible architecture that governs how you interpret reality, make meaning, and decide what to do, long before your willpower ever gets involved. It is the world you believe you are living in.

Every enduring philosophy works this way. **Stoicism** is a thinking system. **Kabbalah** is a thinking system. They do not tell you what to want; they tell you how reality works, where your responsibility lies, and how alignment is restored when life feels distorted.

**GOLD**—my thinking system—functions the same way. For a long time, I was deeply frustrated. I had insight. I had self-awareness. I had ambition in recovery, and yet, I still found myself leaking energy, reverting under pressure, and reproducing results that did not reflect what I *knew* to be true. What I lacked was not discipline or enlightenment. I lacked a system. Now, there is one.

**WHY "GOOD ENOUG**
**DEVELOP AND CAN**

For many reading this boo
land as relief but as threat.
but because their nervous s
ty, belonging, and continuit
that staying vigilant, impre
included.

High-achieving people
bition or preference. In rea
strategy formed early in life
fluctuated, attention was inc
performance, self-sufficiency

In those conditions, a 
language does: *Who I am is*
*to secure my place.* That conc
character; it is the birthplace
sion of you that learned to o
to manage perception, to stay
that looks impressive enough

The problem is not that t
tually outlives its usefulness,
original conditions have chan
that slowing down will cost yc
still be defended through effor

This is why, for so man
strangely unsafe, why stillness
the invitation to simply "be e

# G — Good Enough

*"Self-love isn't everything, but without it, you have nothing."*
GLORIA STEINEM

When I was twenty-four, I was set up on a date with a man everyone assured me was *a very big deal*. A CEO. Powerful. Important. The sort of man I was meant to feel lucky to be seen with. Somewhere between the appetizers and the second glass of wine, he leaned across the table, placed his hands on my waist, and silently assessed my body the way one might inspect a horse before purchase. Then he leaned back, visibly unimpressed, and proceeded to speak to me as though I were already an inconvenience.

And I stayed.

Not just for that date, but for *another*. I did eventually walk out midway through the second, which, at the time, I considered progress. Now, I recognize it for what it was: far too much time to offer a man who had already told me everything I needed to know.

I share this not because it is unique, but because it is painfully common. Most of us can summon our own version in seconds—the job we accepted for far less than we were worth, the relationship we tolerated long after it revealed its contempt, or the room we shrank ourselves to fit because we were so relieved to be invited inside at all. These moments rarely announce themselves as self-betrayal in real time. They arrive disguised as pragmatism, humility, patience, or being "easygoing." Only later do they

register for what the
selves to be enough.

This is why we b

Not because it i
because, without it, t
lieve themselves to b
come enough in the
impressively, and app
beneath all that com
life. Nothing is chose
cess, and even joy are
rather than received.

This is not a mor
beneath you is unstab

When enoughne
You do not trust life;
You do not light up; yo
life well lived. It is the
upon it will feel precal
from the outside.

In this section, we
anchor you in the lived

**No More Countin**
save, complete, or valid

**Assume Everyone**
are disliked, judged, or
assumption that you be

Once enoughness b
life can finally be lifted.

peace. The system is not broken; it is simply loyal to an outdated rule set.

Beneath this loyalty is often a core wound, not trauma in the dramatic sense, but a deeply internalized meaning that says: *If I stop proving, I disappear; if I stop striving, I am exposed; if I stop earning, I am no longer held.*

This book is not devoted to excavating that wound in detail; that was the work of *Gilded*, and deeper identity-level healing belongs in dedicated containers. But it is essential to name it here, because without naming it, the idea of "good enough" remains philosophical rather than lived.

Freedom does not come from convincing yourself that you are worthy while still organizing your life around earning, performing, or being chosen. It comes from installing new rules that make worth non-negotiable and safety internal, so the system no longer has to hustle to survive.

Again, that is what **Good Enough** is about. This section provides a structural reset designed to dismantle the old conditions under which worth was earned and replace them with a way of moving through the world that assumes legitimacy.

# *Anti*-Rule 1
# Stop Counting on Them

*"To trust oneself is the hardest thing, and the most necessary."*
RAINER MARIA RILKE

Intuiting George Costanza's "religion" of doing the opposite, Muhammad Ali also learned this when he refused to be drafted into the Vietnam War. The rule was clear. So was the cost of breaking it. By withdrawing his obedience, Ali demonstrated the first *anti*-rule: Freedom begins the moment you stop cooperating with a system that requires your self-betrayal. Every *anti*-rule that follows in this book will ask you to do something counterintuitive. This first one, however, matters more than all the others combined, because it represents a base pivot: a total reversal of our natural operating system.

Before you can live freely, boldly, or truthfully, you must reverse the habit of orienting yourself around other people's opinions, comfort, and consensus. **You have to stop counting on them**, not out of rebellion or indifference, but to begin trusting yourself again.

Most of us have been trained—explicitly and implicitly—to *count on them*; to read the room, anticipate reactions, manage expectations, secure approval, avoid exclusion, and time our truth for maximum palatability.

We call this being smart, strategic, or considerate. In reality, it is how we outsource authority over our own lives.

If you've ever seen the movie *JOY* (starring Jennifer Lawrence), you know exactly what I mean by "counting on them." The film tells the story of Joy Mangano, the real-life inventor of the Miracle Mop. She was, by all accounts, earnest, hardworking, and smart. She was a dutiful daughter and wife—perhaps too dutiful—always fulfilling her family's needs and demands above her own until one day, things went too far.

After a spill caused by her father's callous new wife, Joy was forced to mop the floor with an inadequate mop, resulting in severe cuts to her hands. After healing from the terrible wounds, Joy arose with newfound revelations and inner resolve, determined to prevent further injuries to herself and others caused by useless cleaning contraptions. She then created her own self-squeezing mop—the first ever—a contraption that would infinitely help her and countless other housewives (and, perhaps, a few capable men as well).

Her rise would not be instant. Though the idea was fantastic, Joy found herself surrounded by doubters. Family members who thought she was naïve, business partners who dismissed her, and people who couldn't see her vision. Growing more and more tired of needing their approval, Joy made her own way, going directly to the producers at home shopping network QVC.

Many people would have folded under the weight of so many inquiring eyes and the underhandedness she encountered right off the bat, but Joy didn't. Instead, she marched into the studio and insisted on demonstrating the product herself. That one decision, no longer counting on *them* to validate her, trusting her own inner knowing that she could sell this, that this product was excellent, got her the QVC stage.

The mop was promptly picked up, sold out, and the rest is history.

Actually, the rest is where all the naysayers, seeing her success, suddenly changed their tune and hoped for a piece of the action. Somehow, Joy rose above this too, finding her path to greater business heights and even familial healing. This reinforces a belief I've had confirmed again and again in coaching others: Master knowing your own worth, and you will become the tide that lifts all the boats. With one important note:

Do not tell them what you are about to do. Do it *first*. Count on **you**.

## OLD PATTERNS DIE HARD

When I launched my coaching career, I spent the first year (okay, first *years*) not taking my own advice. I was obsessively counting likes, refreshing Instagram, tallying clients, and silently wondering after each launch whether the programs were as awesome as I thought, basing my opinion largely on how well they sold. After all, if they didn't approve of me with tangible pings, who was I to call myself a good coach?

That dependence nearly broke me, until I realized that waiting for consensus is the fastest way to kill originality. If I had kept counting on agreement, I never would have stood apart in a saturated industry, never would have charged what I charge, never would have created the programs I knew to be of greatest value, and never would have written this book. The moment I disentangled from applause, I began to move forward and have some fun.

Dependence on the opinions of others runs rampant in our society. The question that reveals where your dependence on others' opinions lives can be found quite easily in probing your pride. Ask yourself what you are proud of. Then ask what it takes to maintain that pride. For example, if you are proud of your net worth, what happens when you find yourself surrounded by people of far greater wealth? Or what happens when someone accuses you of being a greedy elitist, of having more than your fair share, or of jumping above your station?

And what about weight or your overall appearance? If you are proud of the way you look, just ask yourself what your reaction would (truthfully) be if your looks were met not with consensus but with disapproval? If you're thinking, "I'd be just fine," you're either lying to yourself or you're deceased. Even Eckhart Tolle wouldn't fantasize about such a thing. But what Eckhart *can* do is *manage* this impulse—to count on them, and thereby choose a different response, followed by opposite action; proclaiming your allegiance to *you*.

We can afford to give ourselves some slack here. We are human beings, and humans are social animals. We're conditioned to measure our worth by how people treat us. If they flatter us, invite us in, or acknowledge our gifts, then we feel steady. If they withhold those things, then we spiral like a teen pop star.

This is where mindfulness—the simple act of pausing and looking clearly at what is—becomes essential. Because the truth is, sometimes people simply do not have the capacity to give us what we're craving. And if I may be blunt: It isn't their job to do so.

When you expect others to love, validate, or affirm your worth into existence, you set everyone up for disappointment. But if you slow down in the moments when your confidence wavers based on their approval, you can find your way back to yourself—inside your own mind.

The opposite move is to let them off the hook, so you can stop counting and be your own Joy Mangano.

## THE SCOURGE OF COMPARISON

As dispiriting as it is to count on others for approval, it is equally corrosive to monitor them as your competition. Few habits undermine freedom more efficiently. Personally, I think that counting on others is simply comparison in disguise. Consider this: If you are waiting for their approval, you are living inside *their* frame of reference, trapped in the narrow cage of "*What will they think?*" instead of on the far steadier ground of "*What do I want?*"

The absurdity of this arrangement becomes obvious the moment you look at it plainly. Imagine Madonna in the 1990s obsessively tracking Prince—studying his numbers, borrowing his silhouettes, and tempering her instincts to match his genius. The very idea borders on tragedy. Had she done so, we might never have received *Ray of Light*. The world would have been poorer for it.

My own life would *suck*.

Fortunately, history offers more generous models. There are individuals and institutions who paid no attention whatsoever to the competition and were rewarded not merely with success, but with distinction. Taylor Swift did not win by outrunning her peers; she won by refusing to audition for anyone else's role. Hermès does not react, rush, or reposition. It waits. And by waiting, it becomes inevitable. Comparison, by contrast, is always reactive. It produces imitation, not excellence. And while imitation may earn you a seat at the table, it has never once secured a legacy.

## TAYLOR SWIFT

Taylor Swift's success is indisputable. As I write *GILT FREE*, her *Eras Tour* has become the highest-grossing tour in history, surpassing the billion-dollar mark and redefining what scale looks like in modern music—an achievement that even Madonna, in her commercial prime, never reached in a single tour.

How did Taylor get here? Not by tracking competitors, chasing trends, or optimizing for virality, but by building her business entirely on her own terms. As books like Kevin Evers' *There's Nothing Like This* illustrate, Taylor's true genius lies in staying rigorously in her own lane and, in doing so, becoming a category of one.

She has never tried to win the pop game by volume, spectacle, or algorithmic dominance in the way artists like Justin Bieber were structurally designed to do. Taylor, by contrast, has built her career around authorship, narrative control, and long-term audience trust. She writes her own material, she rerecorded her catalog to reclaim ownership, she builds eras rather than chasing hits, and she treats her audience not as a market to be captured but as a relationship to be deepened. The result is durability, not just fame; compounding loyalty, not just reach. This is what happens when strategy is guided by self-definition rather than comparison: You stop competing for attention and start accruing power.

## HERMÈS

Speaking of categories of one: There is luxury, and then there is Hermès. In studying Hermès as an executive coach and speaker, what becomes immediately clear is that the house offers a masterclass in strategic restraint. Hermès has chosen to be smaller, slower, and narrower by design—producing limited quantities, maintaining French-based craftsmanship at far higher cost, resisting licensing, and declining growth opportunities that would dilute standards.

In doing so, Hermès has achieved something remarkable. They commanded equal or greater esteem than LVMH (Louis Vuitton-Moet Hennessy), the largest luxury empire in the world by revenue. LVMH is a triumph of scale, representing acquisitions, category expansion, global footprint, and growth across dozens of houses, namely Louis Vuitton, Christian Dior, and Tiffany & Co. Hermès, by contrast, refuses the logic of conglomerate dominance entirely. It does not chase market share; it safeguards meaning. It does not explain itself; it enforces an internal code. And that is precisely why comparison between them is meaningless.

Hermès and LVMH are not playing the same game. LVMH wins on scale. Hermès wins on integrity of strategy. And in a world obsessed with expansion, Hermès proves a quiet but radical truth: Restraint can outperform growth, patience can beat power, and the most enduring brands are built not by watching competitors, but by honoring an internal standard so rigorously that comparison becomes irrelevant.

These examples demonstrate that when you stop trying to prove, persuade, or win people over, you reclaim energy for what matters—listening to your own inner knowing, aligning with the universe, and saying "yes" to the assignment only you can fulfill. Your Madonna assignment, your

Joy Mangano lightning-bolt idea, your Taylor Swift era, your Hermès-level product, and most importantly, doing all this *your* way.

## BUILDING YOUR INNER CONTAINER (SO YOU STOP COUNTING ON THEM)

Once you stop counting on others for approval, you can expect yet another quirky side effect. The noise in your head quiets, but so does the scaffolding you were leaning on. For a moment, there can be a feeling of exposure, even vertigo; a feeling of disjointedness, like losing your center. As if you are replacing the usual noise in your head with a sense that *if I'm not orienting myself around their reactions, their reassurance, their cues... what am I standing on?*

This is the moment where many people mistake freedom for rebellion, or self-trust for isolation. As a result, they either harden and pull away. *Or* they swing wildly to a new cause, a new society, or a new sense of center. I'm here to tell you that you don't need to rebel, isolate, or join a new religion to stop counting on others (certainly not that last one... kind of defeats the point). You need to build something stronger in their place.

## INTEGRATION: TRANSFERRING AUTHORITY BACK TO YOU

Stopping the habit of counting on others doesn't happen through insight alone. It happens through practice. Through repetition. Through small, deliberate moments in which you choose your own knowing over consensus. What you are doing here is not becoming rigid or self-reliant in a brittle way. You are building an inner structure sturdy enough to hold your worth without it leaking through other people's reactions.

These practices are not about improvement. They are about

**jurisdiction.** They teach your nervous system, your mind, and your decision-making apparatus one simple truth: *My approval is sufficient.*

Use the practices below to formalize that shift.

## 1. THE INNER BOARD OF DIRECTORS

This practice originally comes from *Think and Grow Rich* by Napoleon Hill, but we'll modernize it. Instead of asking, "*What will they think?*" ask, "*What will my wisest self advise?*" Then, create a short list of inner mentors, real or imagined. This might include your future self, a trusted teacher, a spiritual source, or an archetype who embodies self-trust (Joy Mangano belongs here). When you feel unsure, consult these inner mentors instead of polling the crowd.

## 2. THE 24–HOUR PAUSE

When a decision feels cloudy because you're anticipating other people's reactions, wait.

Give yourself twenty-four hours before replying, committing, explaining, or posting. Use that time to journal, walk, meditate, or simply sit with the discomfort. Most clarity arrives once the static of imagined judgment fades.

## 3. THE "WOULD I DO THIS ALONE?" TEST

Ask yourself: *If no one clapped, approved, or even noticed, would I still want to do this?*

If the answer is yes, proceed.

If the answer is no, notice where you're acting for applause rather than alignment.

## 4. REVERSE THE FRAME

Instead of imagining what others will think if you fail, ask: *What will I think of myself if I never try?*

This shifts the decision from approval-seeking to self-respect; from external judgment to internal integrity.

## 5. THE DAILY INNER VOTE

Each morning, write down one decision, large or small, that you are making for you.

It might be:

*Today, I'm skipping that call to protect my energy.*

Or:

*Today, I'm pitching the idea I believe in.*

This daily vote retrains your nervous system to recognize your own authority as real, sufficient, and reliable.

END OF *ANTI*–RULE 1.

Congratulations!

You are no longer counting on *them*.

You are now counting on *you*.

# *Anti*-Rule 2
# Assume Everyone Likes You

*"How could anybody not like you?"*
HELEN SEINFELD (JERRY'S MOM) TO JERRY
ON *SEINFELD*

This may be an unpopular opinion, but I have never quite understood the appeal of Jimmy Fallon. For years I was deeply intrigued by how, in the span of only a few seasons, he rose from the "*SNL* guy" to the host of *The Tonight Show*. This never made sense to me, because in my mind, Fallon has always seemed more cute than funny. Cute helps, of course, but it does not usually earn you one of the most coveted seats in entertainment.

Pondering this sent me down a rabbit hole, and, eventually, I realized what I had been missing. The real strategy was not cuteness, nor even raw comedic talent. It was Fallon's core belief, or at the very least his mode of operation: He assumed that people liked him.

"Assume they like you" sounds naïve, but it is not. It is elite psychology. It is not asking for approval; it is refusing to preempt rejection. Most people walk into rooms unconsciously braced for judgment, scanning for disapproval, carrying a baseline assumption that others are skeptical, critical, or against them. That scarcity script constricts presence and short-circuits charisma before a single word is spoken.

Flip the premise and something profound happens. Anxiety loosens its grip. Your best self has room to emerge. You radiate a warmth and an ease that others instinctively mirror back. I have learned this firsthand as a professional speaker—show up genuinely ready to enjoy the room, and the room rises to meet you.

This becomes possible for you once you stop counting on others to validate you. If you no longer need their praise and affirmation, you can finally relax around them. That release is where the second *anti*-rule begins: to adopt the Jimmy Fallon keystone and assume that everyone likes you.

In studying his rise, I learned that Jimmy elevated this opposite of our default, insecurity-laced belief system into an art form. When he was twenty-one, still a college student performing in dingy comedy clubs, his audition tape landed on the desk of a young Hollywood agent named Randi Siegel. She called him without expecting much. Fallon answered on the first ring.

"Hi, Jimmy, this is Randi Siegel…"

"Randi Siegel! I know who you are!" he exclaimed.

That one moment revealed everything. Fallon was not star-struck, needy, or trying to prove himself. He was delighted, already at ease, and already assuming rapport. Instead of selling himself, he created connection by presuming it existed. Siegel signed him, and within months, he landed the *Saturday Night Live* audition he had dreamed about since childhood.

At *SNL*, Jimmy repeated the same move. While most rookies treated Lorne Michaels like an untouchable monarch, Jimmy followed a piece of advice from a producer: After every show, go thank Lorne. Week after week, Jimmy crossed the floor, looked his boss in the eye, and said, "Thank you for the show." Not in a groveling way, not strategically, but with warmth, presence, and ease. He could do this because when you assume your presence will be welcomed rather than judged, connection becomes the default. Within weeks, Lorne began pulling him into inner-circle conversations, post-show drinks, and genuine professional trust.

Years later, late-night wars were raging and NBC needed someone they could trust with *The Tonight Show*. While Jimmy was not the sharpest satirist or the edgiest voice, he was the one who had always assumed belonging, built relationships without posturing, and walked into rooms as if they were already on his side. As a result, an entire network of people advocated for him, including Lorne Michaels himself.

Personally, I had to learn this lesson the hard way. For most of my adult life, I walked into rooms quietly thinking, "*I hope they like me.*" Networking events, client pitches, dates. (Especially dates if the man in question qualified as what we might politely call a "catch.") The energy was approval-seeking and subtly anxious. It kept my prices low, my pipeline unstable, my confidence shaky, and my dating life stalled.

The day I flipped it, the day I did the opposite and instead walked into rooms thinking, "*I already like me; let's see if I like them,*" everything changed. Clients stopped haggling. I raised my rates without flinching. Opportunities appeared instead of evaporating. And yes, this was the same shift that ended the dating hamster wheel and had me walking into my first date with my now-husband, Ryan, simply in a good mood and ready to enjoy dinner.

Jimmy's rise, as well as mine, both point to the same truth: Assuming people like you is not arrogance; it is alignment. It is what happens, as Brené Brown says, when you stop measuring up and start deciding that you *belong*.


## THE PART YOU CAN'T SKIP: GROWING A SPINE

*(Why "Assume Everyone Likes You" Only Works If You Mean It)*

Essential clarification:

"Assume everyone likes you" is not a mindset trick, not optimism, and certainly not fake-it-till-you-make-it nonsense. It is the opposite move that's available to you *only* when it is backed by something solid. The moment you assume people like you without a spine (in other words—you just *insist* that people like you), you do not become magnetic; you become performative. False bravado collapses under the first raised eyebrow, the first negotiation, or the first moment of friction because confidence without self-respect cannot hold.

This is the part you cannot skip. Assuming people like you only works when you like yourself first—enough to hold your ground if they do not.

Case in point: I didn't truly assume people liked me, and, as a result, my bravado was phony baloney. Despite being naturally extroverted and raised by parents who were convinced of my universal appeal, my over-achieving tendencies morphed into people-pleasing and quiet insecurity by adolescence.

That pattern followed me through my first marriage, my early career, and embarrassingly into the early years of my coaching practice. Even as my business grew and brand-name clients came in, I underpriced myself, over-delivered, discounted at the eleventh hour "to be nice," and said yes to misaligned opportunities because maybe they would lead to something.

Translation: soft spine, leaky business.

The reckoning came at a mastermind for seven- and eight-figure coaches. Sitting in that room, listening to peers describe their businesses and revenue, two truths landed simultaneously. By skill, accreditation, and client caliber, I was among the most qualified in the room, yet by revenue and posture, I was among the smallest. I said it aloud without ceremony—it was a worth issue. I was still asking the world to tell me my value instead of me simply stating it.

I rebuilt my business on a single premise: If I am good enough, I am allowed to act like it. That shift changed everything. Pricing aligned with outcomes. Sales calls became mutual-fit conversations. I stopped chasing and started choosing. Boundaries became clear and consistent. Within months, the quality of clients improved, my days grew calmer, my team stabilized, and my actual coaching sharpened, because I was no longer trying to earn my place while doing the work.

Owning my worth did not harden me; it relaxed me. That is the paradox. A strong spine allows the shoulders to drop. From there, assuming people like you stops being a gamble and becomes a posture. You arrive open—rather than auditioning—and doors open back.

## PRACTICE
## RAISING YOUR WORTH BY RAISING YOUR STANDARDS

1. **Audit Your Floor**
   Write down the "bare minimums" you've been tolerating in business, relationships, or daily habits. Then flip them. Ask: *Would a luxury brand tolerate this? Would the penthouse version of me?*

2. **Define Your "Do Not Want" List**
   Write down five things you are *done* accepting. Examples: clients who haggle, friends who only call in a crisis, work that leaves me drained, trusting others to do what I should be doing, and partners who do not share the lift equally. This list is the basis of your new set of standards.

3. **Set a Standard Statement**
   Choose one new boundary that raises your floor this week. Example: *"I no longer accept last-minute cancellations without consequence."* Say it aloud until it feels natural in your body.

4.  **Design Scarcity with Integrity**
    Limit access strategically, whether it's office hours, calls, or social media exposure; not to manipulate, but to preserve your full presence when you do show up.

5.  **Rehearse Stillness**
    In your next pitch, date, or conversation, let silence land. Resist the urge to overexplain. Trust your offer, your presence, and your worth to hold.

END OF *ANTI*-RULE 2.

Congratulations. You got the part.

# O — Open

Three years into my self-help journey, I met my now-husband, Ryan. I would not become financially free for three *more* years. In hindsight, I think that all went down pretty fast, but for many high achievers I see in coaching, it is not nearly fast enough.

Freedom does not arrive in one dramatic swoop. And it does not install itself automatically the moment your worth is no longer in question. You cannot simply *decide* to be free by upgrading your self-worth. Gloria Steinem warned us about this already. Insight alone does not liberate us. There is still a crucial stretch of road ahead if you do not want to unknowingly trade one cage for a better lit one. Openness—the second commitment—is what makes the difference between liberation (or staying on the path that pleases you) and relapse.

I often see this moment arrive after a real turning point. Someone leaves a marriage that diminished them. Someone finally stops over-functioning, stops apologizing, or stops negotiating their floor. Their self-respect is intact. Their standards are raised. On paper, everything looks right. And then…

Cue musical score from *Jaws*.

A client once came to me six months after leaving a relationship she had clearly outgrown. She was grounded, articulate, and sounded like she was no longer questioning her worth. You could feel the solidity in her body and hear it in her language.

Yet, I couldn't help but notice that she was also irritable and somewhat impatient. Dating felt impossible, she would say. Certain topics shut her down instantly. When I finally pressed her and asked what she thought was happening, she said, without irony, *"I finally know who I am. I don't want to question myself anymore."*

*Hmm,* I thought. *Methinks thou doth protest too much.*

What she had mistaken for self-trust was self-protection. She had swapped low self-worth (less ego, more trust) for more *ego*—leaving her closed off, rather than open. It was understandable, of course, that she no longer wanted to risk feeling foolish, mistaken, or biased, so she hid behind the semblance of enlightenment. Questioning her reactions felt too close to the old self-doubt she had worked so hard to escape.

It's just that… real worth sounds different. It sounds gentle and open, not rigid. Surrendered, not defensive. Totally cool with still having biases, not perfect.

That is the danger point most people miss. Sometimes, when the worth is still glitchy, our second commitment will be far more difficult to bridge, because we will have defaulted back to **certainty.**

If "G" grounded you in worth—you are already good enough—and if raising your deserve level taught you how to stop negotiating your floor, then "O" asks something subtler: How do you hold power without strain, authority without defensiveness, and confidence without the need to be right? Open is not softness, and it is not passivity. It is strength that does not tense. It is the ability to remain flexible, discerning, and teachable even when your identity is no longer fragile.

We are wired to react, defend, and prove. Our minds crave certainty the way the body craves sugar: fast, comforting, and ultimately depleting. Certainty gives the ego a sense of control—especially after it has learned that control works. Once being right has kept you safe, effective, admired, or in charge, the mind does not easily relinquish it.

Open is the opposite move. It is the choice to own your mind rather than let it run mindlessly. It is the willingness to pause long enough to ask whether your impulse is rooted in scarcity or abundance, fear or curiosity. It is choosing a response that serves your future self rather than protecting your ego in the moment.

This is why openness is not optional once your worth is secure. Without it, high self-esteem hardens into dogma, boundaries become walls, and clarity curdles into moral superiority. With it, power stays fluid, energy stays clean, and growth remains possible—even inside success.

## STAYING OPEN WHEN YOU'RE USED TO BEING RIGHT

For overachievers in particular, openness may be the most counterintuitive and essential gilt free commitment of all. High performers are not undone by ignorance; we are undone by the demand for certainty and by how very much we love to be right. We succeed early by learning quickly, mastering systems, anticipating outcomes, and forming strong opinions that allow us to move decisively through the world. *Being right* has kept us safe, effective, and in control for a very long time. Overachievers are, therefore, uniquely vulnerable to confusing knowing with wisdom.

This is why it is important to ask ourselves, in earnest, whether this is really working for us. Is it delivering the results we want, all this being right?

I saw this pattern so consistently that I once gave a talk called *You Don't Know What You Don't Know*. It resonated not because the idea was novel, but because it named something people feel every day and rarely question: the exhaustion of having to be right to feel safe. *Gilded* asked you to confront that honestly. *GILT FREE* is about teaching you how to live without quietly rebuilding the same structure under a more flattering name.

When you no longer need to earn your worth, the work becomes learning how to stay open. Open to being wrong without collapse. Open to new data without defensiveness. Open to change without interpreting it as threat. And open to reality without trying to dominate it. This is not naïveté, and it is not passivity. It is discernment without rigidity, and a strength that does not need to prove itself.

When you are truly open, you stop mistaking your first interpretation for truth. You notice the story you are about to tell before you commit to it. You create just enough internal space to choose a response that serves your future rather than protecting your ego in the moment. Risk, mistakes, and even failure lose their emotional charge and become information instead of verdicts. Arguments loosen their grip, because you are no longer using them to validate your worth.

This is the bridge from a high-deserve level to real freedom: a quieter mind, a cleaner signal, and energy that can move instead of defend. Master this, and you are no longer dependent on a single breakthrough, a single realization, or a single moment of clarity. You become someone who can stay awake inside success itself, not because you control outcomes, but because you remain teachable when it matters most.

# *Anti*-Rule 3
# Take It Easy

*"Nothing in life is as important as you think it is, while you are thinking about it."*

DANIEL KAHNEMAN

This year, I watched the end of the *Sex and the City* sequel series, *And Just Like That…* Like nearly everyone else of sound mind, I found it godawful. So, when news of the show's cancellation spread across social media, I did what any responsible internet citizen would do. I commented with a single word: *good*.

The reaction to my comment that followed was… *bananas*. Strangers I had never met unleashed fury and personal attacks over a throwaway remark about a television show. The intensity was so outsized it bordered on absurd.

I tell you this trivial story for a serious reason: This is how easily perspective collapses. Even after insight, even after "doing the work," reactivity remains close at hand. The brain inflates the moment, distorts its meaning, and drags us back into urgency and righteousness, dragging us—even post-*Gilded* into "I will show them!" mode. That's how fast you can move from *chill* to *kill*.

This happens to all of us, me included. I confess, political posts occasionally draw me in with such urgency, and it's very hard to resist the temptation to pounce on that comment section, like those strangers did with my reboot de-boot. This happens because of what Daniel Kahneman called the *"focusing illusion,"* or whatever you're thinking about right now feels enormous simply because your attention is locked onto it. In reality, it rarely deserves the grip we give it—political posts included.

This is where *Anti*-Rule 3 begins.

## BEING RIGHT VS. BEING FREE

A client of mine—let's call her Diana—was locked in a fierce conflict with a business partner. She had screenshots, receipts, and airtight arguments. And she was right. After months of fighting, legal costs, and sleepless nights, she was also exhausted, bitter, and depleted. She was winning the argument but losing her peace. Worse, she was pouring her life force into fixing something that had already shown itself to be unsalvageable.

This is the hidden cost of righteousness. First comes fatigue. Then bitterness. And finally, identity. When being right remains a key tenet of who you are, you can't let go. You *must* justify, explain, and perform certainty long after it stops serving you. The armor gets heavier by the day. There is no freedom in it.

Psychologists call this cognitive dissonance. To avoid admitting we might be wrong, we bend reality to protect our self-image. This is not a good strategy, if you wish to be free. Which is why, at a certain point, I asked Diana a simple question: **Do you want to be right, or do you want to be free?**

## THE INVESTOR WHO COULDN'T HOLD THE MONEY

Choosing to be chill over being right is not only useful in a litigious situation but in the management of finances, too. If you want a haunting lesson, look no further than the story Morgan Housel tells in *The Psychology of Money* about Jesse Livermore, the legendary stock trader of the early 1900s. Livermore was, by every measure, the most brilliant market operator of his time. He made and lost today's equivalent of billions, *four* separate times. At one point he was literally the richest man in the world. And yet, he ended his life bankrupt and alone.

How did this happen? It turns out, Livermore wasn't undone by lack of intelligence or opportunity but by his *mindset*. He was undone by the inability to stop, by the scarcity-driven compulsion to prove he could win again, and again, and again, and, obviously, by continuing to be beholden to the *focusing illusion*. As Housel put it, he had no ability to say, "That's enough." In other words, at a moment of challenge, Livermore couldn't see straight.

As a result, Livermore could manifest wealth, but he could not hold it because holding success requires something deeper than skill or speed. It requires emotional regulation, humility, and a loose grip. It requires the ability to pause, to not need to be right one more time, and to not chase the high of certainty and control.

Housel contrasts him with Warren Buffett, who has compounded quietly for nearly a century; not by chasing the next win, but by letting time and patience do the heavy lifting. Buffett's genius isn't extraordinary brilliance; it's restraint. It's the discipline of flow, of moving with the current instead of trying to outswim it. This is why so many people can attract success but not sustain it. They can manifest the big moment but not integrate it. They can build the castle but not live peacefully inside it. The difference isn't luck; it's openness.

**I want you to hear this, as this may be exactly the thing that kinked your hose again: The moment you grip your wins too tightly, they slip**

**through your fingers. The moment you flow with them, they tend to stay.**

Livermore's story is not a cautionary tale about money so much as it is a precise illustration of what happens when brilliance outruns openness, when skill is not matched by humility, and when momentum is mistaken for mastery. That guy could predict markets, bend probability, and summon extraordinary outcomes, but he could not yield. Warren Buffett's enduring success, by contrast, is not the result of superior insight so much as superior emotional regulation, the capacity to stay open to time, uncertainty, boredom, and restraint without needing to prove anything in the short term, and this is why one man's wealth vanished as fast as it arrived while the other's compounded almost invisibly for decades.

This is the deeper meaning of openness. It is not a state of passivity, nor of complacency, but the acquisition of the discipline of not forcing what does not need force, the wisdom of sensing when the current is carrying you, and when your effort is a form of interference or—to use Law of Attraction parlance—*resistance*. Loosening your grip is the corrective to the overachiever's compulsion to outswim life, to win one more time, to tighten control just when surrender is required, because real freedom and sustainable success are not created by gripping harder but by learning when to loosen, when to trust the movement already underway, and when to allow life's intelligence to do the work you no longer need to do yourself.

## CHILL VS. RESISTANCE

If you've ever been caught in a riptide, you know that instinct is not wisdom. Instinct is an innate, automatic, hardwired survival response (like fight/flight). However, wisdom—much like intuition—is a deeper, often subconscious knowing or insight based on learned experiences, patterns, and complex information processing. It's feeling a calm clarity or hunch rather than an urgent alarm. Instinct is primal and unchangeable (genetic), but intuition is developed, integrating subtle cues and past knowledge for nuanced judgment, guiding growth beyond mere safety.  When meeting a riptide, the temptation will be to err on the side of instinct, making the mind narrow, and every ounce of effort will go into fighting the current head-on.

However, this is precisely the thing that exhausts you and pulls you under. Every lifeguard gives the same advice, and it sounds offensive in the moment: If you get caught in a riptide, **do not fight.** Instead, turn sideways. Let the current move you until you can swim out safely. This works not because of magic but humility. The willingness to accept the conditions you are in rather than the ones *you wish* you were in.

Life works the same way. What feels like strength to the ego is gripping really tight. Forcing, insisting, proving, and doubling down is often resistance masquerading as control. What feels like surrender—basically choosing to take it easy or to just take things in stride—is frequently the first intelligent move you've made in a long time.

I know this firsthand, too. During those years in Switzerland, I white-knuckled a life that looked coherent from the outside and felt suffocating on the inside; a marriage held together by appearances, a career built on performance without alignment, and a smile that took more energy than it gave back. It was a riptide, and instead of turning sideways and just letting go, I decided to resist each challenge, swimming against it as hard as I could, while holding my breath. The riptide ended up beating me.

Oddly, when I stopped fighting reality—the divorce, the move, the career change—I could breathe again. Righteousness braces. A loose grip exhales.


## WHEN THE STAKES ARE SUPER REAL

History offers a stark illustration in the 1911 race to the South Pole between Roald Amundsen and Robert Falcon Scott. It is an excellent allegory of loosening the grip and being chill versus fighting with reality. Though both men and teams were well matched, Scott—a seasoned veteran suffering from a bit of entitlement, fought the environment at every turn. He relied on untested technology, overextending men and animals, and made decisions guided more by pride and appearances than humility. His team reached the Pole second. None survived the return.

Amundsen, who was the same age, but with fewer conquests under his belt, did the opposite. He studied the terrain in advance. He spent six months learning how to walk in extreme cold temperatures from the Inuit. He overpacked and took extremely good care of the men and animals. As a result, he aligned himself with conditions instead of defying them. His team reached the Pole first and came home alive.

This is not a story about courage versus cowardice. It is also not a case for merely being overprepared for the sake of it, as that would sound anti-chill to those who are discerning. It is a story about posture toward reality that relies on wisdom instead of instinct. Scott had ambition and instincts but lacked chill—making him rigidly reject reality and lose his future. Amundsen had the wisdom to prepare *and therefore* had chill. He could bend with reality, and still have a future.


## IN A WORLD WHERE YOU CAN BE ANYTHING, BE KIND

*"Pursuing kindness can sound nice and easy... like a bubble bath. It's not a bubble bath, it's a fire – but when you get there, you can relax and surrender to yourself and to who you are, and allow things in."*
JOHN CHU


"In a world where you can be anything, be kind" has become one of those trite phrases at which we roll our eyes. It's nice on a throw pillow but is promptly ignored when someone cuts us off in traffic. Yet true kindness—the kind that changes someone's day for the better—is neither soft nor fleeting. It is the product of a most advanced mindset and yet it is rarely our first impulse.

When things go sideways, when we feel misunderstood, threatened, dismissed, or wronged, the instinct is not kindness. Like when caught in a riptide, instinct will go straight to "Start thrashing around!" The instinct is to complain, correct, prove, and fight. To be right. To reassert control. To tighten the grip back. This is why kindness is not our default setting. It is a *regulated* one.

Comedian and writer Larry David built an entire career exposing this truth. His genius is not just that he says what everyone is thinking, but that he dramatizes what happens when we *never* override our most reactive impulses. Larry is perpetually right. He is also perpetually miserable. His refusal to soften—to let things go, to extend generosity where it isn't strictly deserved—makes him correct and unbearable in equal measure. In one especially poignant episode on the HBO sitcom *Curb Your Enthusiasm*, he discovers that he is *not* Jewish and begins to behave, well, like a much nicer, stereotypical *non*-Jewish person. He stops complaining, wears shorts, and wishes people a nice day. It's really funny, and the joke works because it's familiar. We all—Jewish or not—recognize ourselves either in his new, overpleasing persona *who performs* kindness or in the original grump that is Larry David.

Being right feels powerful in the moment, which is why, generally, we let our Larry David side take the wheel. This is far more dangerous than David's comedic extravagances relate. Choosing feeling powerful, or in control, over feeling kind makes us cruel, both to ourselves and to others. That connection was named with startling clarity in a viral commencement speech in 2023, when Illinois Governor J.B. Pritzker told graduating students that the easiest way to identify an idiot is not a lack of credentials or education but *cruelty*. Cruel people, he said, mistake aggression for intelligence and domination for strength. Kindness, by contrast, requires far more thought, discernment, emotional regulation, and perspective. In other words, kindness is not naïve. It is regulated, it is advanced, and it is *intelligent*.

Cruelty is reactive while kindness is thoughtful and composed. Cruelty is what happens when being right matters more than being free. This is why "chill" is the opposite move. When you loosen your grip long enough to take it easy, when you stop needing to win every exchange, explain every position, correct every misstep, something subtle—but profound—happens. You gain range not because you are passive, but because you are no longer enslaved to your urges.

The cultivation of kindness, then, is not the starting point. It is the result of real, hard work, or, as director and filmmaker John Chu says, "It is a *fire*." It is what becomes possible once you are regulated enough to choose long-term freedom over short-term dominance. But, as Chu also accurately explained, once your nervous system is no longer hijacked by urgency, and once you no longer confuse control with power, you are free to not only *belong to* you but to *be* you. It's openness instead of ego at work.

Do I even need to mention that studies show that acting with kindness and generosity toward others measurably increases your happiness and psychological wellbeing?

Feel free to get back to me on that.

# REFLECTION EXERCISE: WHERE ARE YOU STILL GRIPPING?

Answer slowly, from the body, not the intellect.

Where in your life are you gripping for control, certainty, or recognition right now?

What are you afraid would happen if you loosened your grip—even slightly?

What is the cost of continuing to grip?

What would a 10% increase in taking it easy look like this week?

Mazel tov! You are no longer fighting the current. Next, I'll show you how to ride it to where you want to go.

# *Anti*-Rule 4
# Ask for What You Really Want

*"You must ask for what you really want. Don't go back to sleep."*
RUMI

Scoring a book deal is always an accomplishment, but after dreaming of becoming an author for more than five years, selling my first non-fiction book, *Gilded*, felt both astonishing and hard-earned. Like many, I always secretly harbored ambitions of becoming a writer. However, I didn't start taking my craft seriously until my mid-thirties when I invested in coaching and eventually became a coach myself. In 2018, a year after launching my flagship program, Live with Enthusiasm, I realized the need for a single reference manual to accompany my clients through their coaching journey, rather than the ten books I was recommending.

That was when I got serious about becoming an author. I read books like *How to Sell a Non-Fiction Book* and *Creative Writing for Dummies*, along with countless articles on securing the right agent. In tandem, I wrote my first draft—cheekily titled *All Your Problems Solved Forever*. Though it wasn't terrible, and I even got an agent, it didn't work out. That ordeal, which lasted about a year, led to *three* years of trials and tribulations, shelving, and picking up the project again, along with a lot of frustration.

Yet, I persevered and allowed the work to evolve. *Gilded* did not get sold, in all, for five years.

**How I did it:**

**I Accepted No Defeat.** Knowing there are no shortcuts, I kept going. Having a great story, coaching skills, and a big audience isn't always enough. A story needs to feel relevant to readers; otherwise, it belongs in a diary, not a bookstore. To understand what readers cared about, I became an even more avid reader and student.

**I Became a Better Writer.** Before I called myself a writer, I was a reader. I read a lot of memoirs, self-help books, and cultural criticism/history books, as my first book was a blend of these genres. I joined writing workshops to learn about the craft, read mentor texts, and other aspiring writers' works. I wrote and revised multiple drafts with various titles; all along the way honing my skills and clarifying my thoughts.

**I Found an Advocate.** Despite my success as a coach, finding a literary agent was challenging. My first agent was lukewarm, and subsequent agents also struggled to sell my work. It took five years to sign with my current agent, a friend of a friend who had transitioned from a book editor to a literary agent. By the time I met her, I was already considering self-publishing. Together, we focused on making the book truly good; we came together because she *got* the work.

**A Miracle Happened.** My book deal came through a conversation my agent had with a fellow editor who demanded to see the manuscript. She loved it, reached out to me, and the deal was done. I liked her direction for the book, loved the deal terms, and was ready. She was the clear winner.

Now, let's talk about how the miracle *actually* happened. It happened by not overworking, not soliciting directly, not insisting that things come in a certain period, not calling every single person I've ever met, and not resisting any modicum of modifying the work but rather by allowing the work to continue ato evolve to the point of actually being ready. All of these new, learned behaviors are the very *anti*-rules I am teaching here.

I've seen others score book deals based on a single viral essay or a provocative title. Good for them but that's not how it usually works. Talent and tenacity, alongside a generous heap of faith and allowing the work to become what it is truly meant to be, win in the end.

So, this next *anti*-rule is here for those who have been pursuing certain results in any department—from a book deal to love to health to success—and still not sticking the landing. This *anti*-rule is about learning how to ask for whatever your version of "book deal" is and getting it.

## THIS IS HOW WE DO IT

Once you stop needing to be right all the time, your inner lawyer finally hangs up her blazer… which should get you your results, right?

Wasn't that this book's promise?

Alas—wrong on both counts. You may be frustrated to learn that not only did this book make no such promise, but that even when your reactivity begins to tone way down and even after your perspective expands significantly, *still*, nothing happens.

There is a reason for this, and for all intents and purposes of where we are now, let's just say that new results take time. The suffering has eased, yes, but the result has not arrived. You're calmer, but you're not expanded; softer, but not yet receiving; more self-respecting, but still watching certain desires hover just beyond reach like a door that's been unlocked but not yet pushed open.

As mentioned in the last chapter, many will interpret the gap—the quiet, the pause, the "not yet"—as evidence that life isn't cooperating; that they're stuck, that all this inner work was a cute spiritual detour and the real world is still the real world. So, they do what they've always done: They tighten back up, they re-enter the courtroom, they start building a case, they shake a fist at the heavens, and they try to force timing, proof, certainty, and guarantees. They are simply still too enthralled, too addicted, to action. So much so that they do not yet allow themselves to imagine, or ask, for better.

Which is why *Anti*-Rule 4 exists. I think it is time to discuss what is happening while it looks like nothing is happening. Because once you do, you are going to stop wasting your energy on frustration and start learning that all energy is like investing in the stock market. Depositing is only the first move. In the hold, your investment magically grows, and as it grows more and more, you can and will learn to trust it, allowing you to ask for more—without apology, without clenching, and without turning it into another performance. And, instead, with trust.

This is where one thinking system will come in handy—the Law of Attraction. I am not only about to employ that old favorite from the spirituality aisle, but I'm going to use the word "universe" in this chapter, too. If that makes you itchy, relax. Think of the Law of Attraction as nothing more than shorthand for the organizing intelligence of life, the human reality that responds to signal, or simply the belief that when your internal state changes, your perceptions and behaviors change, too. The world meets you differently. Whatever language helps you stay open, use that. The only thing that matters is that you stop negotiating with life like it is your enemy, so you can use what you learn to get what you want with such ease and enthusiasm that you become extra kind and extra generous.

Asking isn't demanding. It's signaling *trust. I trust this is available for me.*

Most people think asking is saying, "I want this." But asking—*real asking*—is the moment you become coherent. Because the truth is you are always asking, even when you're silent.

You ask with your standards.

You ask with your choices.

You ask with what you tolerate.

You ask with how you speak to yourself.

You ask with your nervous system—braced or relaxed, defensive or receptive, constricted or open.

That's why so many smart, disciplined, sincere people feel like manifestation—the term used to describe the art of turning thoughts into things—"doesn't work." They are making requests with their words while broadcasting static with their bodies.

They say, "I want love," while bracing for abandonment.

They say, "I want abundance," while rehearsing catastrophe.

They say, "I want the opportunity," while secretly convinced they are not allowed to have it.

That split is not humility. That split is sabotage. If you are ready to let your desire become honest, to let your inner state become safe enough to not only chill more but to *receive* what you're asking for without immediately tightening your grip and demanding proof, you are going to finally get what you want.


## THE MECHANISM

What people usually mean by the Law of Attraction translated into grounded terms, is this:

The state of your mind and nervous system shapes how you perceive the world and how you show up in it. When you repeatedly think about certain outcomes—success, safety, connection, scarcity, failure—you train your attention to scan for confirming evidence. Over time, this changes what you notice, what you expect, and what you believe is available to you.

Those expectations are not neutral. They influence your emotional tone, your confidence, your willingness to take risks, and how you relate to other people. In turn, they shape your behavior, your decisions, and the opportunities you act on or ignore. The cumulative effect of these choices is what people experience as "manifesting" outcomes.

In this sense, thoughts do not magically *become* things. They become filters. And filters determine which possibilities you can recognize, pursue, and sustain.

**So, when people like me say:**

*"Thoughts become things"* what they are describing is the way repeated beliefs condition perception, behavior, and follow-through.

*"Like attracts like"* what they are pointing to is that your emotional state and self-concept influence who you resonate with, how others respond to you, and which environments you remain in.

*"Ask, believe, receive"* is therefore not a cosmic transaction, but a psychological sequence. You name a desire, allow yourself to believe it is possible, and, therefore, behave in ways that make its realization more likely.

Nothing supernatural is required for what we are about to go through. No energy fields need to be invoked. The mechanism is simple, human, and well-documented. Attention shapes action, action shapes outcomes, and outcomes reinforce belief.

*"Ask, believe, receive"* is a mechanism you can use to turn your asks into results. Esther Hicks—also known as "Abraham" (it's a long story)—the foremost Law of Attraction teacher of these times, boils this process down to three moves.

Ask.

It is given.

Allow.

Sounds almost too easy, right? Sigh. If it were truly that simple, nobody would be stuck in the purgatory of insight-without-results. So, let's go through each of these properly.

## THE THREE STEPS

### 1) ASK (BUT FIRST, CHECK YOUR INTENTION)

All your asking begins with desire, which is inevitable. Contrast (your problems, disappointments, friction) is what creates wanting. You don't have to manufacture desire; life will handle that for you. For example, if you do not have a coffee, you will likely wish for one. If you do not have enough money, you will desire more. If you are currently experiencing a lack of aim, you will desire clarity.

Desire is not the hard part. The hard part is keeping the asking ABUNDANT and not full of lack. We have to ask from the right place, because your words are not the broadcast. Your *intention* is.

Scarcity asks sound like this, even when you don't say it out loud:

"I want it, because I'm behind."

"I want it, because I'm afraid."

"I want it, because I need proof."

"I want it so I won't be embarrassed."

When you ask from a place of scarcity, you tend to receive the scarcity-shaped version of the thing, because the signal isn't "I want love;" it's "I am afraid." The signal isn't "I want abundance;" it's "I don't trust life." The signal isn't "I want purpose;" it's "I'm bracing."

Case in point: I wanted to get married when I was thirty, and I *got married.*

Was that a good result? Famously, no.

Without a doubt. I was asking from lack: from the terror of being alone, from the cultural story of what it means to "win," from the fear that I would become the sad, unmarried archetype I'd been trained to pity. I wasn't asking for partnership as an overflow of wholeness; I was asking for marriage as a shield. I did not want love. I wanted proof. And that is how you end up in a gilded outcome that is poison to the soul.

Step one is not merely to articulate the desire. It is to ask:

**Where is my intention for this desire?**

Is it coming from scarcity or abundance?

Am I asking from panic or clarity?

Am I still obsessed with proof-seeking or with creation?

When you stop wrestling reality, when the need is not gnawing at you, you can finally hear what you want. A clearer message is a cleaner ask. And a cleaner (abundant) ask means a better result.

## 2) IT IS GIVEN (STOP RELYING ON YOUR SENSES LIKE THEY'RE AN ORACLE)

From the moment you ask, you should know that there is a virtual concierge—the universe—who has immediately taken your order and fulfilled it but just has not delivered it yet.

This second step will sound very uplifting, of course, but will immediately come up against your senses. Your senses report the past, and that is what you are more likely to believe. You will believe your bank account's present balance over the virtual concierge. You will believe your current relationship status over the virtual concierge.

I get that it will be very hard for realists to get with the virtual-concierge program around here; it sure was for me. Alas, I realized that as long as I was only living by my senses, I would always be manifesting from yesterday. And yesterday's bank account was no longer enough for me. If it is not enough for you either, or any other department of your life is not, go with the concierge.

"It is given" is the rational choice that says: *The path exists even if I cannot yet see it.* This is rational, not only because yesterday's results are irrelevant, but also because whatever you are asking for, the universe already has for you. If you want a new lover, that person is alive and walking the earth. If you want to start a business, the pieces exist, the path exists, and the clients already exist.

The question is not "Can the universe invent this for me?" The question is whether you can keep your signal clean long enough to meet the path without self-sabotage. And by self-sabotage, I mean stop demanding proof and start allowing yourself to just wait for it.

This is where high achievers get allergic to my insistence that they "keep doing the work." They want proof. They want a timeline. They want the dotted line. They want a guarantee. Which not only does not attract what they want but actively repels it.

I want you to know that every time you demand proof, you reveal that you are still clenching. Which means you are not allowing. However, when your faith remains intact in your desire and the virtual concierge's ability to fulfill that desire, you will get to step three.

## 3) ALLOW (STOP HUSTLING IN A PRODUCTIVITY COSTUME)

Allowing is the step overachievers misunderstand the most because "allowing" sounds like doing nothing, and doing nothing sounds like death. But allowing does not mean passivity. Allowing means coherence. It means that you trust what you desire is already out there, and you are worthy of it. Once you alow, you will stop broadcasting a split signal to the universe. A split signal is a thought with a BUT:

"I want it… but I'm worried."

"I want love… but not like *that*."

"I want money… but it's very rare and a bad thing to want."

A split signal produces static, and static cannot call in a symphony. The moment you broadcast static, you default to your oldest strategy: *making* things happen. Which, if we're being honest, is often just fear in a productivity costume.

Going back to the concierge analogy: If you are staying at the Four Seasons, and you want a coffee, you just pick up the phone, speak clearly to the concierge, and trust the process. After placing the call, you don't pace the marble floors as if your anxiety will expedite the reservation, right? You don't run downstairs to check if they are making your coffee, right?

The energy that will carry you through step three is not only your ability to ask clearly and to believe you are worthy of what you want, and that the universe has it, but to also have complete faith that it's coming. So, you can chillax.

And that's when your results start to land, and land, and land.

## STORIES FROM THE FIELD: WHAT ALLOWING FEELS LIKE

When I met my husband, Ryan, it wasn't a lightning bolt. It was an *of course.*

By the time I met him, I had become quite adept at using the previously described formula, having already successfully launched my coaching business. And so I had asked the universe super clearly for Ryan—from abundance and not from the desperation of yore. I had stopped treating weddings like a non-negotiable treaty requiring some kind of hostile takeover and started treating them like what they are: not relevant in the dating era.

My business was doing well, and I was very happy. For a relationship, I had cleared space in my life—not theatrically, not superstitiously—practically and emotionally, because I wasn't begging to be chosen anymore; I was preparing to receive what I had already decided I was available for. That is why I say when we came together, it was an *of course.* When he arrived, with a big dog and a pile of spare boxers, it felt normal. Not "finally." Not relief.

It was more like: *Oh. There you are. I've been expecting you.*

Same with business. Even though we started, like many businesses, doing well enough to survive—there were a couple of years when a strong month would have sent me into champagne and shrieking. But I stuck with my protocol—getting better and better at steadying my reactions, focusing my thoughts, and stating greater and greater desires, as we continued to grow.

One year, we closed a single month with ten times the revenue that would have once felt impossible. When we did it, there was no champagne. It was me in my bathrobe, high-fiving my Director of Operations on Zoom. Not because I was ungrateful but because good had become normal. Just as with Ryan.

That is what allowing feels like: not fireworks, but familiarity.

It is very important that you know this. So many overachievers live for fireworks. But hear me out: You do not want fireworks. They do not last. You want the steady, chill frequency—that is the match to the ease, the wealth, and the love you desire. Nothing that freaks you out or that makes your heart race can last.

## IN-BETWEEN *ANTI*-RULE 3 AND *ANTI*-RULE 4

*Anti*-Rule 3 taught you to stop wrestling with life.

*Anti*-Rule 4 teaches you what to do once you're not wrestling: **Ask cleanly and allow cooperation.** It is the same move, deepened. You're no longer in the courtroom; you're at the concierge desk. All you have to do is ask.

## GRATITUDE: THE GATEWAY TO SURRENDER

One powerful tool to help you stay focused—without slipping into desperation—is gratitude.

Gratitude is not a journaling gimmick, though it sure seems to be making many people rich on Amazon. Gratitude is a form of signal training and something I highly recommend you become a pro at. At first, you may only be able to lift small weights; walking around, day in and day out, saying thank you for coffee, thank you for my body breathing through the night, thank you for one good conversation, one moment of peace—all inside your head. This will be enough. But if you dare to practice and start expanding, it's important to include things that you would not normally feel grateful for like having a sick cat. You can choose to feel grateful for the ability to help your beloved cat, for the love you have for this creature, and for the eventual recovery. If you do this, you will become a black belt in manifestation. For example, here's some of what I have been grateful for in years past:

- *Thank you for the book not yet published.*
- *Thank you for the soulmate not yet arrived.*
- *Thank you for the abundance not yet visible.*
- *Thank you for this crisis; I bet I will learn something here.*

In Judaism, this attitude of gratitude is captured in one word: **dayenu.**

Dayenu means "Anything we get, it is enough."

Enoughness is gratitude; this is not an endpoint. It's a stance. It is the decision to live as if the path and everything on it is exactly what we need as it unfolds. That stance is oxygen to manifestation, because it loosens the grip, settles the body, and turns all things into coherence and into the very vibration we need to match the things we want.

## DEVELOP EXPECTANCY (THIS ISN'T MAGIC—IT'S MECHANISM)

It is fashionable to dismiss manifestation as woo, but to wrap this chapter, I want to double back and say that we are shifting your expectations here. As an overachiever, whether you know it or not, you have *not* always expected to win (sorry; see *Gilded*), but you *have* always expected to have to work very hard for things and to live up to the expectations of others. But now, your desires and preferences are running the show, and you can afford to move your expectations to ease and flow,  instead of to more to hard work and punishing standards. You can also expect to potentially have way more fun and make way more money, too.

You *can* shift your expectancy, and expectancy quietly steers outcomes through attention and behavior. When you change your inner state, you change what you notice. When you change what you notice, you change what you pursue. When you change what you pursue, you change what becomes possible.

Positive emotion widens the spotlight of attention; threat narrows it. When your nervous system is locked into danger, you can stare directly at opportunity and still not perceive it. When you cultivate calm expectancy, you see more doors and walk through them. That's not spiritual indulgence, it's high-level functioning.

# PRACTICE
# MICRO-PRACTICES FOR
# MANIFESTATION

Because high achievers crave action steps, here are practices that shift from force to flow without turning into a vision-board cliché.

**Emotional reset before action.** Before you send the email, pitch the idea, make the ask, take three slow breaths and ask: *Am I aligned or am I anxious?* Wait until you are aligned.

**Opposite impulse experiment.** Once a week, do the opposite of what you might normally do by canceling a meeting, declining a pitch, leaving your phone at home, or taking a nap. Watch what opens up.

**Daily desire check-in.** Each morning, write one sentence: *What do I genuinely desire today?* Then act from that.

**Embodied visualization.** Don't just picture the outcome, rehearse *the feeling* now. Drop your shoulders. Unclench your jaw.

Let your nervous system learn it is safe to receive and go into *of course* mode. That *of course* stance is the signal the concierge is waiting on—a clear indication of your expectancy.

**Track the quiet hum.** Each evening, jot down three "quiet hum" moments: coincidences, support, ease, right timing. Train your mind to recognize flow instead of scanning for danger. Remember, there is no magic involved here. Training your focus and conditioning yourself to expect certain things makes you more likely to find and sustain them.

## REFLECTION & JOURNALING PROMPTS

Enjoy responding to the reflection questions below. Don't rush through these. Instead, let your nervous system catch up to your intellect.

What have I been trying to force into being and how could I soften instead?

Where am I still sprinting past the view?

What opposite impulse am I willing to experiment with this week?

How do I feel in my body when I imagine my desired outcome is already here?

Which small, daily practice could steady me most right now?

What evidence of the quiet hum have I already seen in my life?

How would my work, love, or wealth look if I trusted timing?

Pause after each question to feel, not think.

## THE REAL ENDING: THE END OF *ANTI*-RULE 4

If you take nothing else from this chapter, take this:

Manifestation is not an achievement, and it is not a performance. It is a state, and that state is only available to someone who has loosened their grip on reality enough to let reality cooperate.

You do not manifest by fixing circumstances first. You manifest by changing your internal weather, acting from it, and then letting the world respond. Asking, in its truest form, is not demanding. It is declaring. It is aligning. It is allowing yourself to want what you want without shame, without panic, and without the exhausting habit of arguing with life as if life must be convinced.

This is where *Anti*-Rule 4 ends: not with giving up your desires, but with finally letting them reach you.

END OF *ANTI*-RULE 4.

Go manifest with enthusiasm.

# L — Lit Up

For a long time, I thought exhaustion was just the price of adulthood.

My first marriage felt like an energy leak I couldn't locate. Nothing was *wrong* in a way that could be pointed to cleanly, yet everything required effort: conversations, decisions, presence. I was constantly bracing by monitoring tone, managing mood, and anticipating fallout. Love, if that's what it was, came with a low-grade hum of vigilance. I mistook that hum for passion. Or responsibility. Or commitment. In truth, it was depletion.

The same was true of my career at the time. Each morning began with a small negotiation: how much of myself would I have to override to get through the day. I dragged myself to the office armed with caffeine, competence, and a kind of grim resolve. I performed well. I achieved things. I was applauded. And I was tired in a way that sleep never touched.

Then, slowly and quietly, those structures fell away.

What replaced them was not fireworks. It was something subtler and far more telling. I fell into a love that does not siphon energy but returns it. I wake beside someone who does not require management, justification, or armor. And I built a career that, more often than not, greets me in *pinch-me* mode. Work that asks for my full intelligence and gives something back to me in return. Not adrenaline. Not validation. *Energy.*

And that is how I learned that once you stop fighting life, while life does not immediately leap to reward you (sorry, most manifestations take time), it *does* begin to instantly return something you may have forgotten you were missing: energy. Not the frantic, caffeinated energy of ambition and alarm, but a steadier, more civilized current.

You are about to wake up *interested* and eager for the day.

When you are interested in what you are doing, you will find yourself making decisions with greater discrimination about how you spend your time not because you should, but because you now possess preferences again. The constant internal debate inside you will start to quiet, more and more. The background exhaustion will lift, just enough for you to notice that something essential has been restored.

This is what being **Lit Up** actually feels like.

It may not be as euphoric or as dramatic as, say, manifesting a lottery win, but it feels like clarity. Like being internally switched on, which is way better than before.

Being lit up is not something you summon through effort or manufacture through willpower. It is what remains once exhaustion, obligation, and fear are no longer subsidized. It is the surplus that appears when force finally exits the system. When you stop bracing against reality, stop negotiating your worth, and stop asking for what you want as if you must justify the request, energy returns to its natural circulation.

Life force, no longer spent on vigilance, becomes available for creation.

At this stage, something else will also become non-negotiable. You will begin to insist—without fanfare, explanation, or apology—on operating, mostly, in your "Zone of Genius." In case you have forgotten what this means, in *The Big Leap,* psychologist Gay Hendricks describes the Zone of Genius as the place where your deepest joy and your highest contribution meet. It is where eagerness overrides duty, where reverence replaces grind, and where service flows without depletion. When you are lit up, this zone does not feel lofty or aspirational; it feels obvious. You know in your body when you are in it and when you are not. You can feel the difference between effort that enlivens and effort that erodes.

To live lit up is to live fully charged, aligned, enthusiastic. Not trudging. Not enduring. Not "making it through the week." But awake, alert, and internally coherent. You are no longer dragging yourself toward your life;

your life begins, instead, to meet you.

This section marks the ignition point. The moment where shedding turns into expansion. Where alignment stops being an interior exercise and becomes a visible orientation of your life and work. If this feels exciting, good. It should. You are no longer learning how to stop leaking energy. You are learning how to direct it.

**A quick word before we go any further:**
One of the most reliable ways people promptly and prematurely *extinguish* this newly restored energy, almost as soon as it appears, is by unconsciously returning to the very game they thought they had outgrown: *the game of comparison*. This happens because, like Livermore, the assumption that something better exists somewhere else (scarcity) is still alive inside your mind. When that happens, the next assumption is that what is present cannot possibly be enough. In other words: bye, gratitude and bye, new *anti*-rules.

A brilliant episode of *Frasier* called "Door Jam" illustrates this. In it, Frasier and Niles receive a misdelivered invitation to an ultra-exclusive day spa aptly named *La Porte d'Argent*: the Silver Door. Instantly, they are giddy with anticipation and, having fraudulently acquired an invitation, elbow their way in. These classic sitcom characters, Frasier and Niles, *live* for access. They thrive on the thrill of being admitted where others are not. To them, this door represents the pinnacle of refinement, achievement, and arrival. The metaphor, it must be said, is almost too perfect (someone give those writers *yet another* Emmy!).

Once inside, basking in their good fortune, they encounter an unforeseen complication. There is another door. A *platinum* door. Behind it, they can only imagine, lies something even more exclusive, even more exquisite, and from which they are being politely, but firmly, excluded. Their delight curdles into agitation. If there is a higher tier, then surely the one they occupy cannot be sufficient. Their enjoyment evaporates. The spa is forgotten. All attention shifts to the door.

What follows is their inevitable attempt to breach it. They succeed, of course. And discover that the platinum door leads directly to the dumpster.

The joke, beyond the physical comedy, is not merely that Frasier and Niles end up in the trash. It is that they never enjoy the spa at all. They are so preoccupied with the possibility of a better experience that they miss the one they are having. Niles and Frasier, status-obsessed as they are, have confused access with fulfillment, once again. In doing so, they extinguish the very pleasure they were so desperate to secure.

This is not a story about status. It is a story about orientation to share with you the disclaimer: You cannot *stay* lit up if you are always lunging for the next latch. You cannot remain energized while scanning the room for the upgrade, the better version, the higher tier that will finally validate your presence where you already are. The way to stay lit up is not to avoid doors altogether, nor to insist on passing through every single one. The way to stay lit up is *to stop playing the game of doors* and to notice: I am already here.

If the point is joy, freedom, and aliveness, then notice—even in brief moments—that you already have them. From that recognition, gratitude is restored, allowing something remarkable to become possible—the re-stabilization of your energy. From that state, your Zone of Genius becomes not only accessible but sustainable. This is the discipline of our next commitment: being *lit up*. Not chasing what glitters or mistaking proximity for progress but by learning to remain present with what genuinely enlivens you and allowing your life to organize around that orientation rather than around the anxious pursuit of the next door.

# *Anti*-Rule 5
# Align First, Do Anything Else After

*"Work hard on what comes easily."*
JAMES CLEAR

After years of inner practice, untangling ambition from worth, and loosening my grip on outcomes, I didn't "optimize" my life or launch a grand reinvention—though I think that may be the lore. I just started directing my attention toward flow. Flow is a state you can attain by doing something you love so much that time stands still for you when you are engaged in it. What I got was not a plan but a mood. Flow produced steadier, more generous internal weather. That mood was a byproduct of doing what already delighted me: reading, studying, and thinking deeply about human behavior. I found myself immersed—*for long stretches of time*—in psychology, self-help, business books, and documentaries. Not because I thought it would lead somewhere, but because it felt nourishing to stay there.

That attention sustained itself. One book led to another. Curiosity turned into study. Study turned into accreditation. Accreditation turned into coaching. And coaching almost immediately became a business. It was lots of fun and felt very organic, unlike the linear and painfully effortful advancements of my younger years.

This is the part we usually get backward. We assume freedom should be used to *force* a new direction. In reality, freedom reveals what you can stay with. Alignment shows you what doesn't require discipline, because it already has devotion built into it.

This is how it often works when people stop self-betraying.

Cases in point: Julia Child didn't "manifest" a culinary empire. She fell in love with cooking while living in France, enrolled in culinary school in her late thirties, and stayed absorbed long enough for mastery to take shape. Ina Garten didn't chase celebrity. She bought a small specialty food store in the Hamptons, because it felt right, then learned obsessively, refined her taste, and built a world around what already gave her pleasure. Martha Stewart began with catering, not as a brand, but as a natural extension of her love for order, beauty, and execution. The empire came later.

None of these women started with scale. They started with alignment. With a calm, coherent inner state that could *hold attention* without strain. From there, effort became efficient. Energy compounded instead of leaked.

That is what alignment is: a good, undivided inner mood where your thoughts, emotions, body, and intention are no longer pulling in opposite directions. It's what it feels like when nothing inside you is arguing with the direction you're about to take.

So now that you have felt energy return, the real question is not "*What should I do next?*

It's "*What can I stay with, gladly, without self-coercion?*"

The answer is not effort.

It is not strategy, scale, or speed.

The answer is alignment. And once you have it, you can do almost anything—*after*.

## EVERYTHING IS A WIN WHEN THE GOAL IS ALIGNMENT

When you are aligned, everything else becomes easier; not because life becomes simple, but because resistance stops draining your energy.

I have lived entire chapters of my life in quiet resistance—like when I was in that marriage and job, both of which felt like being trapped in a gray box. Because of these experiences, I know what living out of alignment feels like, and, chances are, so do you. It is a life very busy watching the clock and numbing; too busy to think clearly about what you want for long enough to actually go do it.

Today, I *feel* first and then do. As a result, I now write, speak, study, and interact for a living. I have reversed the order between thinking and doing. I align my thoughts and mood first and do second. It sure makes the time go faster.

That is the difference alignment makes. You stop burning energy on resistance. You enter states of flow where time dissolves, where engagement replaces endurance, and where work gives energy instead of taking it. Paradoxically, this is where productivity explodes.

Ease multiplies results, because you *like* what you are doing. How about that?

## WHAT ALIGNMENT ACTUALLY LOOKS LIKE

When stripped of mysticism and platitudes, alignment is not a vibe, not a vision-board outcome, and not a spiritual bypass. It is—in scientific terms—known as a state of **flow**. Flow is one of the most rigorously studied experiences in modern psychology.

The late psychologist Mihály Csíkszentmihályi coined this term and devoted his life to understanding why some moments feel alive, timeless, and deeply satisfying, while others feel fragmented and draining. What he discovered was precise. In his definition, flow is a state of complete absorption in an activity where self-consciousness dissolves, time collapses, and effort gives way to engagement—not because the task is easy, but because it is exactly matched to your capacity. Not so simple that you become bored. Not so overwhelming that you feel anxious. But challenging in a way that stretches you voluntarily toward something meaningful.

In flow, attention sharpens. Energy organizes itself. The activity becomes intrinsically rewarding, or what psychologists call an "autotelic experience." It's rewarding not because it leads somewhere else, but because it is worth doing in and of itself.

As Csíkszentmihályi wrote, "The best moments in our lives are not the passive, receptive, relaxing times… the best moments usually occur when a person's body or mind is stretched to its limits in a voluntary effort to accomplish something difficult and worthwhile."

This dismantles one of the most persistent myths about alignment: It is synonymous with comfort. It is not.

Safe bets produce security. Sometimes prestige. Occasionally wealth. They rarely produce aliveness. Books are a perfect example. For most authors, writing a book is financially irrational, emotionally demanding, and wildly uncertain, and yet people continue to write them anyway. Creation does not originate in safety. It originates in alignment.

## GENIUS, FLOW, AND THE WILLINGNESS TO "WASTE TIME"

Jerry Seinfeld, a man who built a fifty-year career and billion-dollar fortune on writing jokes, television shows, and stand-up specials, once remarked that the best way to live is to "waste time doing what you love doing most." He was not offering a productivity hack. He was naming a diagnostic: What you willingly *waste* time on, without applause, reward, or coercion, is almost always a clue to your genius.

Genius, it is important to note, does not mean rare intelligence or exceptional talent. It is the intersection of what you are naturally drawn to, what you are unusually capable of, and what gives you energy rather than consumes it. When you orient your life around that axis, something fundamental shifts. You stop forcing momentum. You stop negotiating with yourself. You stop needing discipline to compensate for misalignment.

This is also where many people panic, because it contradicts how most of us were raised. We were taught not to trust enjoyment—not to build lives around what we love but rather around what pays and proves responsible.

Yet, again and again, the evidence contradicts this training. Alignment does not mean abandoning responsibility. It means upgrading the operating system from which responsibility is carried.

## FLOW AS THE GATEWAY TO THE LONG GAME

Once you can access flow reliably—not as a fluke, but as a state—ambition stops feeling frantic. Scale stops feeling threatening. Bigger goals register not as demands on your worth but as invitations to deepen devotion.

This is where many people falter. They touch alignment, feel lit up, and immediately revert to old habits: forcing, hustling, rushing, as if flow were a reward rather than a foundation.

Flow is not the *prize*, it is the engine.

This is where Jim Collins' **20-Mile March**, a concept from his book, *Great by Choice*, becomes essential. The march is a daily, steady, sustainable pace toward your vision, regardless of conditions and without the obsession with the finish line. Freedom, without direction, drifts. Discipline with too much attention on outcomes breeds resentment. But discipline rooted in flow becomes devotion, which becomes possible when you start monitoring satisfaction instead of the distance remaining to your goal. Satisfaction is your indication.

Satisfaction is not the prize you chase; it is the signal you follow toward achievement. In the Law of Attraction, what you feel is not decoration, it is direction. Satisfaction is the indication that you are on track.

Flow state—doing something you are totally engrossed in and satisfied by—is no longer your escape from the gilded cage. It is the fuel for perpetual flight.

# EXERCISE: THE GENIUS DIET

1.  **Audit and Eliminate**

    *Ask:* Where am I operating in competence, or even excellence, but not genius?

    *Action:* Write down at least three tasks. Circle the ones you will delegate or say no to. Add completion dates and the names of those you've delegated to for accountability.

2.  **Reclaim What You Love**

    *Ask:* What do I love that I've been minimizing or apologizing for?

    *Action:* Rewrite it as a strength. Share it aloud with someone this week.

3.  **Double Your Aliveness**

    *Ask:* What would a 100% increase in energy and joy look like?

    *Action:* List five moves. Choose one. Calendar it today.

4.  **Name the Extraordinary Goal**

    *Ask:* What one goal would make the next three years

extraordinary?

*Action:*

List ten tangible steps.

Name five people who could help.

Reach out to one of those people this month.

You now have the correct fuel

in the manifestation car and, at last,

you know how to steer.

# The Bridge
## *A Reminder of Why We Are Here*

This book, like every great Taylor Swift song, also has a bridge. It's the part that feels different from everything that came before—not because the song is losing its way, but because it's about to return to the chorus with more truth. This chapter lives in the space between *Anti*-Rule 5 and *Anti*-Rule 6, and it exists for a moment almost no one warns you about: the moment after alignment, after the breakthrough, when something real has shifted. And yet it doesn't hold the way you thought it would.

When this happens, it is not because something has gone wrong.

It is because no one told you that expansion requires a different internal skill set than striving. Once the old pressure system disappears, the nervous system does not automatically know how to stand upright in open space. The machinery that once kept you moving—urgency, proving, self-coercion, fear of falling behind—has been dismantled, but with no replacement.

In my coaching work, this is the moment people whisper about, if they admit it at all. It is a secret shame point for those who have done real inner work and are "doing better" by every visible metric, yet find themselves quietly shaken either by their own success or by its sudden, unsettling sense of impermanence. They assume the unease, the slipping back, or the strange feeling of being stuck again means they misread the signal, skipped a step, or failed to integrate the lesson properly, when, in fact, they are encountering something entirely new.

What they are actually experiencing is not collapse; it's threshold.

Up until now, the work has been about opening—loosening the grip, disentangling worth from effort, learning how to stop fighting oneself and life in order to finally allow movement. Once life responds, once space appears, once desire meets reality, a different question emerges, one that is far less discussed and far more consequential.

## HOW DO I LIVE HERE NOW?

*Anti*-Rule 6 exists precisely for this moment. Not as a callback to discipline culture or effort-as-worth thinking, but as the stabilizing force that allows expansion to become livable. Consistency here is not about pushing harder or doing more; it is about creating enough rhythm, containment, and reliability that the nervous system no longer feels compelled to recreate pressure simply to feel oriented.

Consistency, in this framework, is not the opposite of freedom.

It is what allows freedom to last.

# *Anti*-Rule 6
# Screw Talent, Choose Consistency

*"As boring as it sounds, 90% of success is doing the obvious thing for a bizarrely long amount of time, without convincing yourself that there's a shortcut."*
STEVEN BARTLETT

Nowadays, from the outside, my life looks somewhat glamorous and adventurous.

I run a seven-figure global speaking and coaching business. I have clients all over the world. I host a big podcast. I'm on my second book. I'm happily married. If you squint, it looks like a montage: airports, stages, conversations, and ideas traveling fast.

Here is the less cinematic truth: My life is mostly a routine. I wake up. I work. I think. I read. I write. I coach. I move my body. I eat familiar food. I repeat myself more than I surprise myself. And, every two weeks, I take a plane somewhere to do the same things in a different city.

There are very few dramatic plot twists. Most days—brace yourself—feel pretty ordinary.

This used to worry me. I thought something must be wrong. Surely a "successful" or "aligned" life was supposed to feel more… *thrilling*? Surely, if I were doing it right, inspiration would be constant, momentum would be effortless, and novelty would be baked in, wouldn't it? Then I noticed something important: Everyone whose work I admire tells the same unsexy story.

Jerry Seinfeld has spent decades insisting that his life is aggressively routine. He wakes up. He writes jokes. He tinkers. He repeats. His entire comedic worldview is built on the premise that greatness hides inside the mundane, not the exceptional.

More recently, Taylor Swift—fresh off a world-dominating tour and the release of what many (meaning: me) consider her best album, *The Life of a Showgirl*—has been going out of her way to tell people how boring she is. Her training schedule? Three hours of running while singing. Her off-stage life? Traveling with her cats. Baking sourdough. Sewing. Being at home with Travis Kelce. The biggest pop star on the planet, openly devoted to routine.

You know what? I believe her.

This is the part no one wants to sell you: Alignment does not lead to a permanently elevated state. It leads to a life that *works*. And lives that work are built on repeatable structures, not emotional fireworks.

Which brings us to the moment that arrives shortly after alignment—one few people anticipate and even fewer are prepared for. Once the inner weather clears, once you stop fighting yourself, once energy returns and life begins to feel lighter and more cooperative, we expect to be carried forward on a steady wave of inspiration.

Instead, what arrives is something far more ordinary.

It's another *Tuesday*.

Another morning.

Another opportunity to show up or not. This is not a failure of alignment. It is the test of it.

The danger at this stage is subtle. It is not burnout or collapse. It is the temptation to believe that because things finally feel good, they should now move themselves. That inspiration should replace structure. That clarity should absolve you from repetition. That gratitude should exempt you from the unglamorous work of continuing.

But alignment does not eliminate action. It changes the *quality* of it. What you are learning now is how to move again—not from pressure, not from proving, not from fear of falling behind, but rather from a steadier, more sustainable place. This is not a return to hustle. It is the cultivation of something far more protective: consistency that preserves your lightness rather than erodes it.

This is the part that feels backward for high achievers. We assume consistency requires more discipline, more grit, more white knuckling. In fact, consistency is the move that removes intensity from the equation. It replaces heroic bursts with something far more radical: repeatability.

The goal is no longer to push harder. It is to make forward motion so ordinary it no longer requires emotional negotiation.

That is the work and the point of *Anti*-Rule 6—it's to state, for the record, that just as excitement is not the thing, motivation is not the thing, either.

So what is the thing? Consistency.

## MOTIVATION IS A SPARK, NOT A STRUCTURE

Motivation is like an insurance plan with a big brand name and terrible reputation. It is flashy. It arrives in bursts. It loves a clean start date and a dramatic playlist. It makes excellent promises and terrible plans. It is useful at the beginning of things and almost useless everywhere else.

What few people tell you is that motivation is not a renewable resource. It spikes, it fades, and it does not consult your long-term vision before disappearing. If you rely on it as your primary engine, you will find yourself perpetually restarting rather than building.

This is not a character flaw. It is a design flaw.

Real lives are not powered by excitement. They are shaped by what you are willing to repeat when excitement is gone. Fictional case in point:

There is a moment in *Hacks*, Season 1, Episode 6 ("Tunnel of Love"), that captures this distinction better than any productivity manual ever could. Deborah Vance (played by Jean Smart), a veteran of the Vegas comedy circuit, watches her young, brilliant writer Ava spiral into self-pity. Ava is undeniably talented and furious that the world has not yet recognized it. She wants her voice heard now, on the strength of her brilliance alone. To my delight, Deborah does not comfort her. She does not motivate her. She asks one devastatingly practical question:

"Talent? Talent is just the price of entry. Everyone here is talented. What else do you have?"

That question is the dividing line between potential and longevity. Between wanting the life and being willing to live it. Talent may open the door, but it does not keep you in the room. Something quieter, sturdier, and far less glamorous is required.

## WHEN MOTIVATION FAILS (AND IT WILL)

Years ago, I tried to adopt someone else's "perfect" routine in pursuit of a gilded outcome. On paper, it was flawless: famous-person diet, famous-person workout, famous-person schedule. For four days, I was convinced I was glowing: thinner, calmer, morally superior.

Then on the fifth day, I got tired, I got hungry. By the sixth day, I found myself at a party, devoid of willpower, stuffing myself with rosé and cheese. I did not last *a week*.

Why couldn't I stay motivated? Was I that much weaker than said influencer?

Nope.

My motivation didn't fade because I lacked discipline. It faded because the goal I was pursuing was not actually mine. The routine I borrowed was not built for my body, my energy, my values, or my real life. It was cosplay. And when you build your life around someone else's goals, using someone else's system, your nervous system will eventually revolt. You will "lose motivation" not because you are lazy, but because your body knows it is wearing a costume it never consented to wearing.

This is the part we tend to misunderstand: Motivation is not a reliable internal resource. It is inherently unstable, because it is often propping up something inauthentic. When the desire underneath is borrowed, performative, or driven by comparison, motivation has nothing real to anchor to. In that sense, motivation is not only unreliable—it is frequently a lie.

Lasting motivation, when it appears at all, is a *byproduct* of genuine interest—not a substitute for it. Your clear and true desire generates motivation; motivation does not generate desire. This is why waiting for a lightning bolt rarely works, but stacking small, honest wins inside a structure you can live with almost always does. Something shifts; not emotionally, but structurally. That shift brings us to the real point.

## WHY CONSISTENCY PROTECTS ALIGNMENT

Consistency is not about grinding harder; it is about **protecting and sustaining the state of flow—aligning with your true desires.** When you are aligned, your nervous system is no longer braced. You are not running on adrenaline. You are not fueled by urgency or fear. That is precisely why returning to erratic, inspiration-based action is so dangerous as it reintroduces instability into a system that has just learned how to rest.

Without consistency, alignment becomes fragile. You feel good one day, scattered the next. Grateful in the morning, resentful by evening. The highs return, and so do the crashes. Consistency creates a container. It allows your system to trust that it does not need to panic to produce. It replaces drama with rhythm. And rhythm, over time, becomes safety.

## CONSISTENCY OVER TALENT, SYSTEMS OVER GOALS

Once you see motivation clearly—not as a virtue, but as a byproduct—the solution becomes obvious. While your talent is useful, consistency will be the true go-getter around here.

For consistency, what you need is not more talent, nor bigger goals, but **systems.** A system is a repeatable process that produces a predictable outcome. If your system is "work when inspired," you will work far less than you think. If your system is "at 9 a.m., I write for 60 minutes, no matter what," you will ship more than your former self believed possible—and without the emotional whiplash.

This is where consistency stops being about discipline and starts being about design. You are no longer asking yourself to feel a certain way to move into action. You are creating conditions that allow action to occur even when feelings fluctuate, as they inevitably will. Which gives me a chance to share yet another—*and* my favorite—Jerry Seinfeld story with you.

In the '70s, when Jerry was coming up on the comedy circuit, he did not have an Ava-from-*Hacks* moment. His realization was quite the opposite. He recounts realizing very quickly that his talent would not get him far, as nearly every comic he met was very, very talented. What he understood then, instead, was the key to success and longevity would be a reliable means to write new content every day and every year—so he could stay in the game.

That has become his big secret—the "Seinfeld System" for creating long term:

Commit to writing every day for two hours.

Then, get a big wall calendar. Each day you write, put a red X on the date. After a few days, you will have started a chain of Xs.

Your job is not to break the chain.

That's it. That is the whole system.

Notice Jerry's system makes no demand for brilliance, for anything to "go viral," or for producing *usable* material each day. All his system requires is *showing up and doing the thing.* This tiny ritual shifts pressure off the moment and onto the system. And, as Jerry's fifty-year winning streak demonstrates, systems *compound.* Design one that fits your life, and you will not need to brute-force change. Your identity will shift on its own, as will your results. You'll notice another side effect: mastery—the getting better, day after day.

That is what Deborah Vance was talking about in *Hacks.* She was correct.

## NO SHORTCUTS

Malcolm Gladwell popularized the ten-thousand-hour principle for a reason: You cannot binge your way into mastery. It is built through repetition, feedback, and course correction—AKA the boring middle.

The good news is that, once earned, mastery cannot be taken from you. The hours are banked. The skill lives in your body. This is why trends do not rattle professionals. They have something no algorithm can erase.

## REFLECTION
## CONSISTENCY OVER TALENT

Where have I been waiting on inspiration instead of designing a repeatable system?

What is the smallest version of my practice I can do on my worst day?

Which environmental change would make consistency easier?

If I never relied on motivation again, what would my week look like?

In six months, what identity would I be proud to claim because I earned it?

END OF *ANTI*-RULE 6.

Hooray! You are no longer waiting to

feel ready. You *are* ready.

# D — Devoted

## AMBITION, WITH A MORAL CENTER

At 4:12 a.m., before the city remembers its name, a baker named Rosa ties on her apron in a quiet kitchen that smells faintly of yesterday's cinnamon. There is no audience. No phone balanced against a jar to capture a time-lapse of dough becoming bread. No applause waiting on the other side of the work.

Alone, Rosa weighs flour by feel because she's done it ten thousand times. She adds water that's neither cold nor warm but just right. She turns the bowl with the heel of her palm, and the dough answers back the way a friend nods when you've said exactly what needed saying.

It's not glamorous or tedious. It's glorious.

When the timer dings, Rosa doesn't check her phone. She thumps the bottom of a boule and listens for hollow music. She adjusts the next mix. She repeats. By the time the first customer drifts in at 8:03 a.m., sleep still clinging to his eyes, Rosa is already complete. Day after day. Not because anyone is watching, but because the work itself demands devotion.

Devotion is not intensity. It is not sacrifice. It is not discipline for its own sake. **Devotion is sustained, skillful care offered without self-reference.** It is what happens when the work, the practice, or the people in front of you matter more than how you are perceived while doing it.

You may be relieved to learn that not all devotion happens at 4 a.m. in a quiet kitchen. Sometimes, devotion happens later in the day in a dark room pulsing with Broadway beats in my favorite place to begin the day: SoulCycle. I am not religious, but SoulCycle is where I go to pray. Surrounded by strangers on bikes, sweating and breathing in rhythm, I'm reminded that devotion can be collective, too. That a hundred hearts can pound in sync not for applause, and not even for self-improvement, but because the practice matters. Because we showed up, and we all chose to begin the day together.

Anchored in effort and presence, making that same choice every few days starts to feel like choosing the right orientation toward life.

This is the heart of the **D** in **GOLD.**

You've grounded yourself.

You've opened your mind.

You've lit up.

Chances are, your results are going to begin to pour in any day now. Now comes the part that makes it all last.

Devotion is what turns inner freedom outward; into habits, service, standards, and care. It is where enoughness and gifting are married into something sturdier than mood or motivation. In this section, we uninstall the old firmware that demands urgency and spectacle. We replace it with a new operating system that chooses consistency over crisis, standards over vibes, and presence over performance.

At first glance, devotion can sound like a return to obligation, especially if you have spent years disentangling yourself from duty, people-pleasing, and the quiet belief that your life exists to serve everyone but you. I want to be clear from the outset: Devotion is not the opposite of belonging to yourself. It is what becomes possible only after you do.

Ultimately, devotion is where the work stops being dramatic and starts being real.

A brief word before we dive in.

The itch you might feel in your teeth right now—the part of you that wants the surge, the sprint, the big reveal—deserves acknowledgment. The part that wants to be undeniable, impressive, and chosen. That part is not your enemy; it's just young. It learned ambition in a culture that taught it to point inward, to ask: *What do I get? How do I look? Does this count?*

Give it a hug. Thank it for getting you this far.

And then let it rest, because this is not the end of ambition, but it *is* the end of **pointless ambition**—the kind that feeds on comparison, applause, and self-reference. The kind that burns hot and fast and leaves nothing behind but exhaustion and optics. That ambition is toxic not because it aims high, but because it aims only at the self. It confuses motion for meaning and intensity for impact.

Devotion does not cancel ambition; it turns ambition outward and redeems it. When ambition is for service—for the loaf that feeds a neighbor, the class that steadies a room, the work that lifts a standard for everyone who comes after—it stops being corrosive and starts being catalytic. Ambition, rightly ordered, is simply devotion with a long horizon. It is the willingness to keep showing up, to get better on purpose, to shoulder responsibility not for glory but for contribution.

This is the quiet revolution. Ambition that no longer asks, *Will this make me special?* It instead asks, *Will this be useful? Will this help? Will this last?*

That kind of ambition does not spike and crash. It compounds. It builds trust. It builds skill. It builds people. And over time, almost mysteriously, it builds results that look a lot like success—only cleaner, calmer, and far more satisfying.

## ONE FINAL, QUICK WORD BEFORE WE DIVE IN.

High achievers would do well to watch out for *hubris*. Hubris, in Greek tragedy, is excessive pride toward or in defiance of the gods, invariably incurring their wrath. Caution, lest you trip up the universe: Devotion curdles into hubris the moment it forgets its source. When devotion becomes identity—*I am the devoted one*—it quietly turns back into ego. Standards harden into superiority. Consistency turns into righteousness. You stop serving the work and start defending your self-image.

True devotion remains teachable. It stays in relationship. It listens. The moment you become unable to correct, devotion has already slipped into dogma. If you ever feel the old hunger stirring, don't suppress it. *Aim it.* Give it a direction worthy of your life. Let devotion be the container that holds your fire steady, so you can keep the promises that matter—not just to yourself, but to the world that needs what you offer.

# *Anti*-Rule 7
# Pass the Tests

*"What you resist, persists. What you accept, transforms."*
CARL JUNG

The first time I watched the mahjong scene in *Crazy Rich Asians*—the penultimate scene where Rachel Chu deliberately throws the game instead of going in for dominance—I felt a quiet click in my chest. That single move contains the entire jam of manifestation, distilled into one elegant decision.

Rachel is playing against her potential future mother-in-law who has made it painfully clear that Rachel does not belong. The stakes are enormous. Win the game, and she proves herself. Lose, and she confirms every doubt. And yet, Rachel *chooses* to lose. She throws the game.

Not because she doesn't know her worth. But because, for the first time, she does.

By throwing the game, Rachel makes something unmistakably clear: She is not opting out because she fears rejection. She is opting out because she refuses a life that requires endurance of quiet contempt. She is walking away not from love, but from the need to prove. She releases the chokehold on outcome and becomes entirely unbribable.

This is not retreat.

It is not defeat.

It is sovereignty.

This is what passing a test looks like when it is powered by a statement of your self-respect. Not "I don't care." Not "I'm above desire." But something far more precise.

## I REFUSE TO ACCEPT A PARTIAL WIN

At this level of life, chill is not enough. You need wisdom. The ability not only to ask, trust, and allow, but to surrender. And surrender, as it turns out, has been wildly misunderstood.

Surrender is not letting go of the desire. It is letting go of the suffering around the desire.

It is the shift from forcing to allowing, from bracing to breathing, from "prove it" to "I'm ready." Only someone who knows they are enough can afford to entirely put down the false god of possession. And when they do, what arrives does not feel like a lottery win—it feels like what was always meant for them. Only someone who knows their worth plays to win, rather than merely playing not to lose.

All of this sounds lovely in theory. I can practically see you now: hands on hips, chin lifted, ready to stride boldly into alignment. But here's the part most books skip: This stance remains theoretical until you are asked to *hold it under pressure*.

Once you live aligned—truly aligned, not just aspirational—life responds, not with applause nor any other form of instant gratification, but instead with a test. The test is what will either allow that manifestation to reach you or not.

A "test" is not a pop quiz you can cram for nor a final exam with the rules taped to the door. This is a subtler assessment—a test of faith, of whether your desire is rooted deeply enough to survive discomfort, delay, and doubt.

Tests almost always arrive right after you make a real shift. After you stop performing. After you step out of old patterns. After you choose truth over approval. Which is precisely why so many people misread them. They assume difficulty means they've done something wrong.

In fact, it usually means the opposite.

Tests don't show up to block alignment. They show up because alignment has begun.

I've seen this pattern so consistently in my own life and in the lives of hundreds of clients that I now consider it a universal law. When you move toward freedom, the universe does not reward you immediately.

It audits you.

The audit is simple.

*Are you serious about changing your life?*

Are you serious enough to keep going when the light doesn't turn green on your timeline?

Are you serious enough to hold your standards when what's offered is close—but not it?

Are you serious enough to remain aligned when reassurance is nowhere to be found?

That is the test.

And it almost always comes in two forms.


## THE TWO TESTS EVERYONE FACES

The universe rarely tests you with outright failure. It tests you with *almost*. Almost comes in two forms.


### 1. THE DELAY TEST

Nothing moves. No traction. No feedback. You've done the work, sent the emails, shown up—and still, the light stays red. This is where impatience disguises itself as realism. Where fear puts on sensible shoes and calls itself practicality. Where the thought creeps in: *Maybe this isn't meant for me.*

## 2. THE DISCOUNT TEST

Something does arrive but it's quite what you asked for. A job that's adjacent to the dream but underpaid. A relationship that's warm but misaligned. An opportunity that flatters while quietly constricting. It tempts you with relief. What it asks is this: *Will you betray yourself just to make the waiting stop?*

These tests are not punishments. They are calibration points. They reveal whether your desire is rooted in alignment or in desperation.

No one illustrates this more clearly than one of my favorite fictional heroines: Miriam "Midge" Maisel of *The Marvelous Mrs. Maisel.*

And unlike Rachel Chu, Midge doesn't pass the test once.

She passes it again.

And again.

## MIDGE MAISEL AND THE ANATOMY OF A TEST

If you've seen *The Marvelous Mrs. Maisel,* you already know the arc. If you haven't, here's the distilled version: Midge goes from polished Upper West Side housewife to comedy legend, but not by being discovered early, rewarded quickly, or spared humiliation.

Her rise is paved with setbacks. Her husband leaves. Her finances collapse. She's blacklisted by powerful men. She lands a dream opportunity and loses it in a single night. Again and again, the door opens just enough to give her hope and then slams shut.

What matters is not that Midge perseveres. It's *how* she perseveres.

She refuses gigs that violate her standards, even when she's broke. She chooses long-term integrity over short-term relief. She keeps refining her craft even when the industry punishes her for it. She does not collapse into bitterness nor does she contort herself into palatability just to make the waiting end.

Midge does not pass the test by being rewarded quickly. She passes the test by refusing to abandon herself and quit—as most of us do—when reward is delayed. That is the *anti*-rule.

## WHAT A TEST FEELS LIKE

What makes tests so destabilizing is not their difficulty, but their *texture*. Tests rarely feel dramatic or cinematic. They don't arrive with trumpets or villains. They arrive quietly, in the gap between effort and response. In the pause after you've done the brave thing and expected movement—only to find nothing happens.

Inside a test, the nervous system begins to buzz at you a bit. Not loudly at first. Just enough to be distracting. Your body tightens. Your mind scans for proof. You start replaying conversations, rereading emails, and rechecking numbers. You feel foolish for caring so much and restless for caring at all. There is often a low-grade embarrassment to it—a sense that you are somehow behind, exposed, or missing a memo everyone else received.

Being in a test can feel humiliating, especially for high performers who are used to the correlation of effort in, outcome out. Tests break that contract. You do the work but nothing moves. Or worse, it feels like something moves *slightly*, just enough to tempt you into self-betrayal.

This is when the urge to *explain yourself* appears. To justify your timeline. To soften your standards. To tell a story that makes waiting feel less uncomfortable. You may feel compelled to stay busy, not because there is anything intelligent to do, but because stillness starts to feel like failure.

Physically, tests often show up as agitation. Tight shoulders. Shallow breathing. A buzzing restlessness that sends you scrolling, emailing, tweaking, adjusting—anything to relieve the discomfort of not knowing.

Since this discomfort is internal and largely invisible, it's easy to misinterpret. People assume they're losing motivation, losing faith, losing their edge when what's happening is that they are being asked to tolerate uncertainty without abandoning themselves. This is the skill tests are designed to build.

That skill is endurance, not in the traditional sense, but more in the steadiness and "keep your eye on what matters to you" sense. The ability to stay present, aligned, and self-trusting when reassurance is absent and results are delayed. To resist the urge to force resolution just to soothe the nervous system.

Tests don't ask you to be heroic. They ask you to be honest and to be still. In other words, see previous *anti*-rules.

## HOW HIGH PERFORMERS FAIL TESTS (WITHOUT REALIZING IT)

Most people of a high-achieving disposition don't fail tests by giving up outright. As usual, they fail them quietly, convincingly, and with very good reasons. High performers are especially skilled at this, because they've been rewarded for adaptability, responsiveness, and problem-solving their entire lives. When something doesn't work, they adjust. When friction appears, they optimize. When discomfort lingers, they assume something must be wrong and that it's their job to fix it.

But, as we have established, tests are not asking for fixing. They are asking for *steadiness*. Here are the most common ways high performers fail tests while believing they are being mature, responsible, or strategic.

### THEY CONFUSE PANIC WITH STRATEGY

The nervous system spikes, urgency floods in, and suddenly every move feels justified, because it's framed as "being proactive." Emails get sent too fast. Offers get revised prematurely. Boundaries get softened in the name of momentum. What's happening is not strategy—just another variety of relief-seeking. And it will not pass any test.

## THEY CALL IMPATIENCE DISCERNMENT

"This doesn't feel aligned anymore," they tell me—not because alignment has shifted, but because waiting hurts. The test becomes unbearable, so the desire itself gets discredited. This is not intuition refining the path; it's discomfort trying to exit the room. I have literally watched people who are *obsessed* with coaching decide, "maybe I am actually not that into it," merely because their first email announcing their new coaching endeavor to the world failed to make them a star. Personally, as their coach, I do not buy it. Neither should you.

## THEY CALL SETTLING GRATITUDE

A partial opportunity appears, and instead of asking whether it truly fits, they shame themselves into accepting it. "*At least it's something. I should be thankful.*" When gratitude feels like relief instead of reverence, it is nothing but a cover for fear—fear that holding the line might mean holding it forever. Don't take the bait.

## THEY CALL QUITTING SELF-RESPECT

This is the most convincing failure of all. Leaving gets reframed as empowerment. Withdrawal gets dressed up as boundaries. And sometimes, of course, leaving *is* self-respect. During a test, however, this move often has less to do with dignity and more to do with escaping the vulnerability of staying. This one is a stance of invulnerability. If you are hitting it, go back to the worth work, because you have a worth issue.

## THEY CALL DISTRACTION REST

Instead of restoring the nervous system so they can reengage cleanly, they numb. They disappear. They tell themselves they're "taking space," when what they're really doing is avoiding the quiet intensity of wanting something without control over when it arrives. That is just old, addicted behavior. Hopefully, they will realize that they have replaced making a decision with seven hours of daily scrolling, and they will get back into the game.

None of these moves look dramatic from the outside. That's why they're so dangerous. They feel sensible. They feel adult. They feel earned. Each one has the same outcome. The test is failed, not because the desire was wrong, but because the person abandoned alignment just so they could feel better quickly.

Passing a test requires something counterintuitive for high achievers: the willingness to tolerate discomfort *without* converting it into action, explanation, or exit. The willingness to surrender.

You can do it.


## MY TEST, AS AN EXAMPLE

At some point, every person in a test hears the same sentence: *Maybe this isn't meant for me.*

This sentence sounds reasonable. Even wise. It often arrives wearing the costume of maturity: *I'm just being realistic.* But make no mistake, this is not intuition. This is the test speaking.

That voice does not ask you to change course because the desire is wrong. It asks you to quit, because the discomfort is high. I remember encountering this voice very clearly in my own life.

At thirty, I sat across from an astrologer who told me very calmly and unapologetically that soulmate marriage would not happen for me until my forties. I nearly choked. At the time, I was frantically trying to manifest a husband. I went on endless dates. I never declined a setup. I dressed strategically at all times, just in case. I pushed, chased, hustled love the same way I hustled everything else.

In hindsight, the astrologer wasn't predicting failure. She was naming a test. And I totally failed it by snapping at her and with everything I did afterward.

I didn't fail because I waited too long. I failed because I refused to wait at all.

I forced a marriage at *thirty* to someone I knew deep down was wrong for me. It collapsed. I forced a career that looked impressive on paper and hollowed me out. It collapsed, too. None of it lasted, because I hadn't passed the test yet. The test was asking me to release urgency without releasing desire. To trust timing without abandoning standards. To stop confusing motion with alignment.

When I finally did, when I stopped forcing and started cooperating with reality, life moved again. Quietly. Cleanly. In its own time. The business I love didn't begin until I was *forty*. My marriage didn't either. When those things arrived, I didn't think *it's about time*. I felt peace.

## YOU'RE MAKING IT WAY TOO HARD

Most overachievers resist surrender, because we were trained to believe control is noble, effort is virtue, and struggle is proof of worth. And, to be fair, it has "worked" for us, at least on paper. But here comes that question again—has it *really* worked?

If your desires still feel out of reach, if your life still doesn't feel as good as it looks, if you're still sprinting past the view, then give surrender a real college try.

Picture it this way: You're holding a cork under water. You've been pressing down so long your arms are trembling. You've convinced yourself this is hard but noble work. But the cork wants to float. If you let go, it rises, doing what it was designed to do.

That is what surrender feels like: not defeat, but release.

## A SHARPER USE OF SURRENDER

By now, you understand that surrender does not mean quitting, collapsing, or resigning yourself to fate. It does not even mean "go back to square one." Surrender simply means: Let go of your egoic control.

Surrender means you stop burning energy on panic, resistance, and story-making, so you can redirect that energy toward clarity and intelligent action.

High achievers struggle here, because effort has historically kept them safe. Slowing down feels irresponsible. Letting go of urgency feels like heresy. But urgency is not devotion. Urgency is fear dressed up as productivity.

Surrender does not ask you to stop. It asks you to stop *forcing*.

When you stop forcing, something subtle but powerful happens. You begin to see more clearly. You refine instead of thrash. You adjust instead of implode. You pass the test not by overpowering life, but by staying aligned long enough for life to respond. This is why surrender is not the opposite of perseverance. It is the intelligent expression of it.

## WHEN THE LIGHT STAYS RED

I see a pattern constantly with clients. There is always a stretch in any meaningful pursuit where nothing seems to move. No response. No traction. No visible reward. This is where most people fold.

They panic. They lower standards. They take the almost-right thing. They quit one minute before the light changes. Then they wonder why manifestation feels elusive. The truth is, the issue is not that manifestation isn't elusive, it's that their desire is conditional. Which brings me to two examples—one public and one deeply ordinary—that illustrate the point perfectly.

## LEANNE MORGAN

At the time of writing this, Leanne Morgan is sixty years old and suddenly everywhere: Netflix specials, sold-out arenas, late-night television, and a major sitcom deal. She looks like an overnight success—if you ignore the previous three decades.

Leanne worked for years in small clubs. She watched peers break through while she stayed grinding. She had deals that fizzled. She had every reason to believe it wasn't going to happen. And yet, she never collapsed into doubt.

When asked what sustained her, she said simply: *"I always knew this was mine."* Not urgently, not desperately, but with complete calm.

She kept offering her work. Letting it deepen. Trusting timing without abandoning herself. And when the world was ready for her voice, it arrived—not early, not late, but clean. Her story is a reminder that timing is not denial. Sometimes it is ripening. If you believe in your talent and in your own capability, let it ripen.

## THE REALTOR WHO STAYED ONE MORE YEAR

A friend of mine is now one of the top real estate agents in New York City. Seven figures. Celebrity clients. Powerhouse career. As many SoulCycle rides as he wants. He has got it MADE. But it was not always like this for him. In fact, in his second year, like most real estate agents, he was broke, exhausted, and ready to quit.

Anyone who understands commission-based industries knows this moment. You're not just struggling, you're bleeding. He couldn't afford basics. The dream felt cruel. And yet, a quiet voice said: *Not yet.*

So, he made a strategic surrender. He took a side job to stabilize his nervous system. He renewed his license. He kept refining his craft without desperation. That decision changed everything. The breathing room created clarity. Clarity created confidence. And momentum followed—very swiftly—in the form of a celebrity client and a million-dollar listing, allowing him to start building a serious book of business that anchors him to this day.

Sometimes the difference between failure and breakthrough is not effort—it's whether you can remain steady long enough to see the green light. I say stay steady.

# PRACTICE
# HOW TO PASS A TEST
# (WITHOUT FOLDING)

When you hit a test—and you will—do this, in order:

1. **Name the moment.**
   Say it plainly: *This is a test.* Not a verdict. Not a failure. A phase.

2. **Rest on purpose.**
   Pause without spiraling. No dramatic decisions in depletion. Let your nervous system settle.

3. **Recalibrate the frame.**
   Ask: *What am I making this mean?*
   Delay is not denial. Almost is not destiny.

4. **4. Adjust one thing.**
   Not the whole plan. One refinement: the pitch, the boundary, the timing, the offer.

5. **Stay for the green light.**

   Do not abandon the path out of impatience. Stay aligned long enough for life to respond.

## A PRAYER FOR THE TEST

When I feel myself forcing, grasping, or spiraling, I return to these words, which are taped to my desk. You may borrow them or rewrite them in your own voice.

*Dear Universe,*
*I see the test.*
*I release the urge to rush and the urge to control.*
*Let me meet this moment with steadiness and offering.*
*Let me rest when I am weary and trust when I cannot see.*
*Let me stay aligned long enough for clarity to arrive.*
*Thank you.*

# REFLECTION
## MEETING THE TEST

Before you turn the page, pause here.

**Name the test.**
Where in your life does it feel like the light is stuck on red?

**Spot the impulse.**
What does fear want you to do—quit, force, settle, run?

**Hold the line.**
What standard are you being asked to protect right now?

**Choose the next clean move.**
What is one small, aligned action you can take—without urgency?

**END OF *ANTI*-RULE 7.**

*Do not quit now.*

*You are about to hit gold.*

# *Anti*-Rule 8
# Don't Be Afraid

*"The greatest enemy of fear is not courage. It is usefulness."*
VIKTOR FRANKL (ADAPTED)

Human beings have always preferred reassurance to uncertainty, even as history insists on offering the latter far more reliably than the former. We wake, pour our coffee, check our phones, and, alas, before the day has properly begun, discover that the rules have shifted once again.

In the last few years, a tool we had never heard of has replaced an entire department. An industry that once promised stability dissolved overnight. A role that anchored identity and income evaporates before lunch. If your stomach tightened reading that, know this: The reaction is not pessimism. It is your nervous system registering change before your mind has caught up.

We are not approaching disruption as a distant possibility. We are already inside it. Change at this scale is no longer a future scenario to prepare for; it is the defining condition of the decade we are living through. Entire professions will disappear not because people failed, but because the underlying game shifted. Skills that once made you indispensable will expire faster than a lease renewal. Capabilities that earned respect and security for decades will quietly stop mattering. None of this is a personal indictment. It is the landscape itself reconfiguring beneath our feet.

The real danger in moments like these is not simply the loss of a paycheck, a title, or a carefully-constructed identity. The deeper danger is the reflex that follows. In times of this much turbulence, even the most grounded among us can revert to base instincts. We cling to what is already dying. We buy bravado over substance. We fold, cave, and bend our values. We outsource agency to anyone who promises certainty again. That reflex is fear, and fear's favorite disguise is conformity.

I have one thing to say to that: *don't.*

The mind has one primary job, and it is not happiness, fulfillment, meaning, or even truth. The mind's job is survival. Survival favors predictability, repetition, and the familiar—even when the familiar no longer serves life. Left to itself, the mind will always default to fear, because fear once kept us alive. The problem is not fear itself. The problem is letting fear lead.

Courage, then, is not something loud or cinematic. It is not the absence of fear, nor the ability to bulldoze through it. Courage is the practiced refusal to let fear run the show. It is the willingness to remain awake when numbing would be easier, to remain flexible when rigidity feels safer, and to move from integrity when conformity offers comfort. This chapter—and in truth, this entire book—has been quietly training you for that stance.

We are living in a century defined not by stability, but by acceleration: technological acceleration, cultural acceleration, and narrative acceleration. The speed itself is destabilizing to the human nervous system. If you find yourself oscillating between panic, resistance, and strategic numbing just to function, do not lose hope. You are responding normally to abnormal velocity.

Throughout history, periods of rapid change have been accompanied by a collective tightening: a turn toward rigidity, nostalgia, and simplified stories that promise order. When societies wobble, fear overwhelms flexibility, and conformity masquerades as safety.

You cannot control these macro-patterns at scale, but you can interrupt them within yourself. When you do, you become something increasingly rare: a flexible, grounded, GOLD human being who stabilizes others not through dominance or sacrifice, but through presence. You do not defeat fear by denying it; you outgrow it by refusing to obey it—and by continuing to serve.

In moments of upheaval, you will meet yourself, and there are two possible responses waiting.

The first is the rigid self who clings to the old story, because it once worked. This is the self who refreshes LinkedIn compulsively, searching for a carbon-copy title that might restore worth. Nights are spent scrolling. Days are spent bargaining with reality. Resentment hardens into identity, and certainty becomes a hunger that is never satisfied.

The second is the flexible self who pauses long enough to breathe and grieve honestly. This self loosens its grip on identity before it calcifies into armor. Instead of asking how to get back what was lost, it asks what this moment might be making room for. It regulates the nervous system before rewriting the résumé. It reaches for people, not for answers, but for grounding. It learns something new, not because it is guaranteed to work, but because staying frozen is the only guaranteed failure.

These are not two different people. They are two different responses living inside the same person. One is automatic. The other is trained. Fear activates the first by default. Courage strengthens the second by practice. *Do not be afraid* is not a command. It is a discipline. The bylaw of this *anti*-rule is to accept what is happening as if you had chosen it. This stance, though not always available, makes life far more pliable.

Pliability—or emotional flexibility—is what we need now. For centuries, mastery meant doing one thing well for a lifetime. You apprenticed, refined, perfected, and passed it on. Identity was stable, because the world was relatively stable. That model is dissolving. Our tools now think with us. Our environments shift faster than our identities can keep up. In a world where the rules change mid-game, the advantage no longer belongs to the most credentialed but to the most adaptable. Emotional flexibility has become the skill of the century.

Emotional flexibility is not passivity or magical thinking. It is the ability to feel fear without letting it dictate behavior, to remain open under pressure, and to pause instead of brace. High-drive personalities resist this more than anyone. When you have built a life on performance, releasing an identity can feel like death. And yet those who thrive are the ones who can release an old way of seeing and learn to see again. This is not self-help. It is survival—more than that, it is freedom.

When I reflect on what flexibility looks like in real life, I think of people not at the moment of crisis, but years later, after fear has had its say and been gently dethroned. I think of the executive who lost her job in a merger and initially scrambled for the nearest replica of her former title. We sat with her panic instead of outrunning it. Only then did she build the consultancy she had quietly dreamed of for years. Today she works fewer hours, earns more money, and chooses her clients deliberately. The business was not the breakthrough; the emotional flexibility came first.

I think of the father who spent decades conforming to an image of success that slowly hollowed him out as it required him, or so he believed, to conceal his sexual orientation. When he finally told the truth, he lost some relationships that were conditional, yes, but he also gained a life that was real. Years later, his children describe him not as perfect but as present.

I think of the physician who retrained into an entirely different field not because she was forced, but because she created enough internal spaciousness to choose. She grieved the old identity before changing the headline. Fear did not disappear in any of these stories. It simply stopped being in charge.

None of these people stopped change. They accepted it and were able to move with it. That fluidity is what we have been aiming for all along.

Want to become fluid? There is one secret: No one adapts alone. Fear thrives in isolation. Community interrupts that spiral. A high-integrity, emotionally-mature community regulates the nervous system simply by existing. This is why I do not just coach individuals; I build containers where people practice flexibility together. Courage is contagious. So is calm.

This is also how societies heal. Trust does not travel at the speed of ideology; it travels at the speed of relationship.

Which brings me to Lieutenant Dan.

For me, Lieutenant Dan from the movie *Forrest Gump* remains one of the clearest fictional teachers of surrender ever created. Dan enters the story with absolute certainty about how his life is supposed to end. For generations, every man in his family has died in war, and that destiny is not something he fears; it is the structure that gives his life meaning.

When ambushed in Vietnam, Dan does not retreat. Instead, he plants himself in the chaos, daring fate to keep its promise, and ultimately losing his legs in an explosion. When Forrest saves him against his will, Dan experiences survival not as rescue but as theft. He is not grieving his legs; he is grieving the collapse of the story that told him who he was.

What follows next is a raw portrayal of what happens when fear hardens into identity. Dan rages at God, fate, and anyone who might explain why life refused to cooperate with his blueprint. He drinks. He isolates. Every invitation to soften feels like betrayal because accepting life as *is* would require grieving what will never be.

Then, quietly, life offers him a second chance disguised as something unimpressive: Forrest offers him a spot on his new shrimping boat, companionship, and a place to show up. Dan hops aboard and his purpose returns, provisionally. Day by day, that purpose grows stronger. By the time a great storm arrives, Dan climbs the mast and laughs into the wind, no longer negotiating with reality, no longer demanding an explanation. He is not fighting the storm. He is inside it.

The next morning, the ocean is calm, and Dan makes peace not with victory but with what is. From that surrender, life begins to move again. The miracle was never his legs. It was that he no longer needed them to stand.

When I stopped arguing with how wrong my life had gone and began meeting it instead, I did not find redemption in a grand reveal. I found it in usefulness. I took an interim job. I volunteered on a suicide hotline. I showed up without insisting that life match the identity I thought I was supposed to be living. Over time, I did not eliminate storms; I learned to move with them.

Fear still visits me from time to time, but it no longer has authority.

I believe the times we live in and are heading toward are harkening our own Lieutenant-Dan moment. We may respond as he did, which would be awesome. For now, we are responding a bit more like Dan 1.0— with excess and denial.

This is par for the course. Eras of rapid change tend to produce extreme reactivity and excess. Every age of excess tells itself the same story: the problem is bad actors, weak laws, or insufficient enforcement. It isn't. The deeper problem is fear allowed to run unchecked.

Take the original Gilded Age of America, a term coined by Mark Twain. It followed the end of slavery and the Civil War—an era of immense upheaval. For decades, the nation swung toward excess, corruption, and unrestrained ambition. That era did not collapse under greed alone; it collapsed under the absence of restraint.

What ended it was not a return to the past or a sudden moral awakening. It was acceptance. A generation born into disorder stopped pretending there was a simpler world to recover. They accepted the reality they had inherited—rich, mobile, diverse, and unmoored—and made a quieter, harder choice. Instead of demanding more freedom, they chose restraint. Not restraint imposed from above, but restraint chosen from within. As external controls weakened, they understood that the only alternative to chaos was self-limitation. Acceptance made restraint possible. Restraint made stability possible.

Acceptance, however, is not the end of the road. Eventually, it must turn outward, into participation. Like Dan found after the shrimping boat. Acceptance makes the road appear.

## COME TO SERVE

On the morning of October 7, 2023, Israeli husband and wife Noam Tibon and Gali Mir-Tibon did what they did most Saturdays: They drove to the coast and went for an early swim in the Mediterranean. Sirens sounded while they were in the water, but they stayed where they were; experience had taught them that, paradoxically, the sea was safer than land during rocket fire.

When they returned to their car and checked their phones, they saw a message from their son, Amir, who lived with his family on Kibbutz Nahal Oz, close to the Gaza border. There were terrorists inside the kibbutz, moving toward their neighborhood.

Noam had served thirty-five years in the Israeli military and retired as a major general. He knew how such situations were supposed to unfold. He contacted senior commanders he knew personally. They told him forces were aware and were "on the way." The phrase unsettled him. Israel's military doctrine is built on speed and presence, and "on the way" suggested something had already gone terribly wrong. Before he had time to analyze the feeling, something quieter and more decisive took over: *This is mine to do.*

They got into the car and drove south, ignoring red lights, the roads eerily empty, the air thick with distant gunfire. At one point, bullets crossed the road ahead of them. Gali slowed the car, the two of them briefly debating whether to turn back, when suddenly a young couple emerged from the bushes—barefoot, shaking, still dressed in party clothes, disoriented, and terrified. They had fled the Nova music festival.

There was no discussion. Noam and Gali opened the doors and pulled them into the car.

Later, Noam would say, "You don't leave anyone behind. It's not a hard decision."

Fear is loud and verbose. It narrates endlessly, weighing risks and demanding certainty before it moves. Service is quiet and sparse. It recognizes obligation and responds. It asks only what is needed now.

They drove the couple to a police checkpoint and continued, passing burning cars, bodies, and scattered groups of soldiers struggling to understand the scale of what was unfolding. Under heavy fire, Noam kept fighting his way forward, then back again, carrying more and more wounded to safety. Gali drove them out through the chaos until she found ambulances. All survived.

Finally at the kibbutz, Noam and Gali moved from house to house, checking doors. A locked door suggested life inside. An open door often meant blood and silence. Nearly ten hours after the day began, they finally reached their son's house. The door was locked. That alone gave them hope.

When Noam called out to them, he heard his three-year-old granddaughter answer, "Grandpa is here." They were saved.

By the end of the day, Noam and Gali, two grandparents, had helped evacuate more than four hundred people.

This is a breathtaking story, but not a story about heroism. It is a story about fear losing jurisdiction. Once the Tibons were given a chance to serve others—with their lives—fear no longer governed behavior. There was no room for ideology, self-pity, or paralysis. There was only life directly in front of them, asking to be met.

This is what service does. It disrupts the endless internal negotiation with reality. It pulls us out of abstract terror and into concrete usefulness. When you are serving—another person, a family, a community, a calling—you stop asking whether life is safe or fair and begin participating in it as it is.

I did not find my way out of fear by waiting until I felt brave. I found it by being needed. I served my clients when my own life felt unstable. I committed to my marriage when retreat would have been easier. I showed up not because I had clarity, but because withdrawal had become another form of fear I was no longer willing to obey.

Service is not self-sacrifice. It is participation. It places you back inside the current of life, where fear cannot dominate, because it is no longer the center of attention.

To serve is to stay devoted to life itself, not to how you wish it would behave. To serve is to accept reality without approving of it. To serve is to stop complaining about what frightens you and start alleviating it.

Service is the final antidote to fear. When fear no longer governs your decisions, love has room to return. Hope returns. The future stops feeling like a threat and starts feeling like a conversation—one you actively participate in.

# FINAL REFLECTION

Before you close this chapter, make it personal by journaling on two questions:

Where are you being called to show up—not to be safe but to be useful?

What fear would lose its power if you stopped waiting and started serving?

Anything you want is already done.

And now you know.

# GOLD — From Gilded to Golden

*"There is no path to happiness. Happiness is the path."*
BUDDHA

I remember almost nothing about my wedding—the manifestation on which I had worked my entire life. How funny is *that?*

I know it was beautiful. The photographs are stunning. Everyone says it was joyful, warm, and effortless. I believe them. But when I try to recall a single, distinct moment—the music swelling, the vows landing, seeing friends, what we talked about, and just about anything but The Hora—I come up mostly blank. The day passed in a blur, so quickly it barely registered.

This is notable because I waited more than forty years for that wedding. My first marriage had no ceremony—just city hall, a quiet legal transaction that, in retrospect, foretold exactly what was missing. So, when I finally married Ryan, this felt like *the* arrival. The long-awaited milestone. The moment that was supposed to land, crystallize, and mean everything.

It *did* mean something, just not what I had been trained to expect. I expected the wedding to be everything. In the end a wedding is just a party. The wedding was gilded, but the marriage is gold.

The ceremony was a moment. The marriage is a decade of ordinary mornings, shared values, laughter, repair, patience, devotion, and deep safety. The wedding was lovely. The marriage is transformative. And no amount of anticipation could have prepared me for the quiet, compounding richness of the thing that came *after* the milestone.

This is *arrival fallacy* in its most innocent form—the belief that peace, fulfillment, or satisfaction will finally arrive once a particular moment is reached. The promotion. The perfect body. The book deal. The relationship. The applause. The proof.

You have already seen how this works. The moment comes and goes. The high fades. The nervous system recalibrates. The mind immediately looks for the next door. Not because you are broken, but because arrival was never designed to deliver what you were asking of it.

The gilded cage was never the problem: It was the agreement you didn't realize you had signed. The agreement that meaning lives in outcomes. That relief lives in milestones. That worth is deferred until further notice. The real turning point was not in achieving something different; it was in questioning the premises on which the deal was offered at all. Let's pause here to take account of what that shift has already changed.

GOLD is not a philosophy, nor a personality type, nor a set of ideals you must perform correctly. It is a cheat sheet: a manual for building yourself from the inside out, into a life that no longer requires fear, force, or self-betrayal. It is the life that becomes possible once you stop outsourcing your worth and stop negotiating with reality. It rests on four commitments that now live inside you, whether you name them explicitly or not.

**G: Good Enough** is where everything begins and where every old story ends. It is the recognition that your worth is not provisional, earned, revoked, or renegotiated based on outcomes. Without enoughness, nothing stabilizes; with it, the floor beneath your life rises. You stop over-functioning and calling it excellence. You stop bargaining with the world for permission to be yourself. From here on, fear is no longer proof.

**O: Open** is what becomes possible once worth is no longer on trial.

You no longer need to react, defend, or control in order to feel safe. You learn to pause, to separate fact from story, to let information replace drama. Discernment becomes your compass, allowing you to move intelligently instead of urgently. Mistakes stop being indictments and start being data. Fear still speaks—it always will—but it is no longer believed automatically.

**L: Lit Up** is the return of aliveness. Focus reconnects to a cause that feels noble, meaningful, or simply true for you. Obligation gives way to enthusiasm. Grind gives way to resonance. Creativity returns. You stop enduring your days and start participating in them. Flow becomes recognizable, not mystical, and alignment stops being an idea and becomes a felt sense in the body.

**D: Devoted** is where everything becomes real. This is where enoughness no longer seeks applause, where flow insists on consistency over drama, and where alignment sustains itself through service to something beyond the self. Devotion does not kill ambition; it refines it. It gives ambition a spine and a soul. This is where your life stops being about what you get and starts being about what you give—without martyrdom, without self-abandonment, and without fear.

Taken together, these four commitments dismantle the illusions that once governed you. You no longer confuse urgency with importance or motivation with devotion. You no longer organize your life around recognition or mistake force for freedom. You no longer panic when consistency replaces excitement or quit when a test appears.

You have learned, again and again, to pass the tests when they arrive, not by proving yourself, but by refusing to abandon yourself. This is why the great traps lose their power here. Arrival fallacy no longer convinces you. Though you may still opt for a big splashy wedding (and you should—the pictures are worth it!), you have by now seen and internalized that the applause fades, the highs crash, and the "next thing" always awaits. You no longer confuse dopamine with meaning or movement with freedom. You understand that if peace is postponed, it is never coming.

Greed, in its quieter form as chronic not-enoughness, loosens its grip as well. When enoughness is real, grasping softens. When devotion is present, accumulation stops being the point. You stop chasing doors for the sake of doors and notice that the life you were waiting for is already here.

What remains is not boredom or resignation, but reverence. A quieter, steadier life that does not require constant optimization to feel meaningful. A life in which fear still arises but no longer governs your decisions. A life lived not in reaction but in relationship. Which makes *you* larger than life.

## REFLECTION
## BECOMING GOLD

1. Where in your life have you already stopped obeying fear, even if quietly?

2. Which old rule no longer governs your choices the way it once did?

3. What feels steadier, calmer, or more honest now than when you began this work?

4. If you trusted what you have already integrated, how might you move forward with a little more ease and a little more love?

# Bye Bye Birdie

*"To perfect this limited self is to forget this limited self...*
*joy is self-forgetfulness."*
ASHA NAYASWAMI

I've alluded to this before, and it bears repeating: Living a gilt-free life is quiet.

This will sound counterintuitive to many people—and weird coming from a coach and motivational speaker. When we say we want to break free, what we usually mean is we want out of stuck and into something impressive: an upgraded life, a bolder chapter, a more cinematic version of ourselves, ideally with better lighting and fewer consequences. Freedom, in this fantasy, still looks like accumulation. It just wears nicer clothes.

What I have found, instead, is something far less theatrical and far more wonderful. Living gilt free is unremarkable in a way that can initially feel almost disappointing—especially if your nervous system was once calibrated to urgency, striving, and the constant hum of self-improvement. When you have spent years equating aliveness with pressure and meaning with motion, stillness can feel like loss. Or worse, like settling.

It isn't.

This quiet is not emptiness; my days are full. They are simply absent of constant worry and negotiation with the future. There is a moment—nothing spectacular—when you realize you no longer experience your life as a problem to be solved. You can finally look around without needing what you see to lead somewhere else. You no longer reach for your phone to feel okay. It is nice here.

The truth I owe you is this: The real sum of my spiritual devotion, now more than a decade deep, has been subtle and mostly internal. It has not been about transcendence, peak experiences, or permanent bliss. It has not been about Birkin bags or first-class flights either—though there was a time when I would have insisted those were, in fact, the point. It has been about my growing capacity to contain life exactly as it is, without fleeing, fixing, or fantasizing my way out of it.

Carl Jung had a name for the state this work ultimately points toward. He called it Sophia—not as a spiritual ideal, but as a symbol of psychological maturity. In Jungian psychology, Sophia represents the highest archetype of the divine feminine principle of wisdom, or the integration of the conscious or unconscious mind.

Jung did not describe this as a spiritual achievement, but as adulthood of the psyche: the point at which we stop arguing with reality and start meeting it. Not with resignation, but with clarity. Not with detachment, but with presence.

You may notice, after putting this book down, that you are less interested in being impressive and more interested in being honest and less concerned with optimization and more devoted to integrity. If so, that is great. It's much more realistic, too.

When I personally consider what remains after the glitter has fallen away, I return to the woman who opened this book. Consuelo Vanderbilt, who was born into extraordinary wealth and extraordinary constraint, raised as a bargaining chip in a transaction she did not consent to, installed into a life of grandeur that functioned, for many years, as a cage rather than a coronation. If anyone had reason to become brittle or embittered by power, it was her. Yet, she did not.

What distinguishes Consuelo is not that she escaped suffering, but that she refused to let suffering curdle her humanity. Beneath the crushing expectations of dynasty and inside a loveless arranged marriage, she slowly transmuted privilege into responsibility, ornament into usefulness, and visibility into service. She became known, not for her title, but for her kindness. This is what a gilt-free life looks like when power does not disappear but matures.

In the end, Consuelo did not transcend her circumstances. She sanctified them. She proved that goodness is not naïveté, and that reverence for life does not require innocence, only integrity. Her evolution—from gilded to golden, from spectacle to service—stands as quiet proof that the highest use of any life, no matter how burdened or blessed, is to leave the world more humane than we found it.

My deepest wish for you—for every reader who has found their way to these pages—is not that you succeed, manifest, optimize, or outperform your former self. It is, rather, that you make it for yourself, and that you are good to the rest of us. That whatever power, money, love, or influence passes through your hands is met with care. That you stay human when it would be easier to harden. And that when life inevitably strips away the glitter, what remains for you is kindness, responsibility, and a deep reverence for being *alive.*

You already left the cage by the time you got here. Now, I hope you ditch it for good.

# Glossary of Key Terms

**ABUNDANCE**

A mindset of trust and possibility—the belief that there is more than enough, and that life's goodness can expand. Abundance feels calm, quiet, generous, and steady. It is the energy behind intuition and true magnetism.

**ALIGNMENT**

The state of being internally coherent; where your values, attention, energy, and actions are moving in the same direction. It feels like a **good mood, like resolve, like clarity—like focus** sustained without force.

**ARRIVAL FALLACY**

The belief that lasting peace, fulfillment, or happiness will finally arrive once a specific external milestone is reached, only to discover that the moment passes and the inner state remains largely unchanged.

**ATTRACTION (THE LAW OF ATTRACTION)**

The principle that your mindset and energy broadcast a "signal" that draws experiences of the same frequency. A noisy or scarcity-based signal repels; a coherent, abundant signal attracts. (See: Esther and Jerry Hicks, *Ask and It Is Given*.)

## CORE WOUND

The core wound is the original break in belonging that gives rise to the persona. It is not the trauma itself, but the moment the psyche decides *who it must become* in order to be accepted, safe, or loved.

As Carl Jung described, the persona is the mask we learn to wear so we can function in the world. It works. It earns approval. It protects us. But it also distances us from the Self.

The core wound is what makes the persona necessary in the first place. Until that wound is faced, insight becomes performance. Growth becomes rehearsal. And even freedom remains conditional—granted only if the mask stays intact.

## SCARCITY

A mindset rooted in fear and limitation—the belief that there isn't enough (time, money, love, opportunities, etc.) to go around. Scarcity drives defensiveness, comparison, and over-efforting. (See: Stephen Covey's *The 7 Habits of Highly Effective People*; Keren Eldad, *Coached* podcast, "The Secret Thoughts of Superstars.")

## FAUSTIAN BARGAIN

An exchange in which one trades integrity, freedom, or soul for external gain—success, money, approval. Named after the legend of Faust, who sold his soul for knowledge and pleasure. In the modern context, it's the deal made when authenticity is sacrificed for achievement.

## FLOW

A state of alignment and ease, described by Mihály Csíkszentmihályi as complete immersion in an activity, where time distorts and effort dissolves. Also connected to Taoist *wu wei*, or "effortless action." Flow feels like life carrying you, rather than you forcing life.

## INTEGRITY

Brené Brown defines integrity as "choosing courage over comfort; choosing what's right over what's fun, fast, or easy; and choosing to practice our values rather than simply professing them." Integrity is alignment between your values, words, and actions.

## OVERACHIEVER, HIGH ACHIEVER

A person capable of intense focus who channels that drive into *trying* rather than simply *achieving*. Overachievers push beyond what is required, not always out of joy or mastery but out of compulsion, perfectionism, or the need to prove themselves.

They may be CEOs, athletes, parents, gardeners, or anyone who takes something "a bit too far." What unites them is not their résumé but their relationship to effort: striving, fixing, perfecting, optimizing, and doing more than is necessary, often at the expense of ease, presence, and self-care.

## MANIFESTATION

The process of bringing desired experiences into form through alignment of thought, belief, and action. True manifestation is less about "wishing" and more about clearing resistance and stepping into coherence. (See: Keren Eldad, *Coached* podcast, "Manifestation vs. Manipulation.")

## MASTERY

Mastery is the sustained, long-term pursuit and embodiment of excellence in a skill, craft, or domain. It goes beyond competence or short-term achievement; it reflects deep practice, refinement, and integration of knowledge until performance becomes both consistent and intuitive. True mastery requires patience, discipline, and humility—showing up repeatedly, learning from feedback, and embracing gradual improvement rather than shortcuts. It is not just about technical skill but also about self-awareness, ethics, and the ability to adapt, teach, and innovate from a place of grounded expertise. And, in this author's opinion, it is the only thing worth "achieving."

## SELF-ACTUALIZATION

A state of fully realizing and expressing one's highest potential, authentic nature, and unique gifts. Popularized by Abraham Maslow as the peak of his hierarchy of needs, self-actualization is not about perfection or status; it's about alignment. It occurs when your outer life (work, relationships, habits) reflects your inner truth and values. In practice it shows up as creativity, integrity, purpose, and a sense of contribution that feels both free and deeply satisfying. The emotional holy grail.

## SURRENDER

Not passivity, but release of control and, therefore, of suffering. Michael Singer, in *The Untethered Soul* and *The Surrender Experiment,* teaches surrender as letting go of resistance to what is, so life can unfold with greater intelligence than control could ever provide.

## ZONE OF GENIUS

Coined by Gay Hendricks in *The Big Leap,* this is the sweet spot where your greatest talents and passions meet, producing work that feels both effortless and impactful. Living here requires letting go of self-imposed limits and upper-limit beliefs.

# Resources


**BOOKS**

- **Keren Eldad,** *Gilded: Breaking Free from the Cage of Ambition, Perfectionism and the Relentless Pursuit of More* (2025)
- **Esther & Jerry Hicks (Abraham Hicks),** *The Astonishing Power of Emotions, Ask and It Is Given* (2004)
- **Tosha Silver,** *It's Not Your Money* (swap "money" for any desire) (2019)
- **Byron Katie,** *Loving What Is* (and YouTube)—for dissolving split focus (2003)
- **Brené Brown,** the complete works
- **Gay Hendricks,** *The Big Leap* (2010)
- **Martha Beck,** *The Way of Integrity* (2021)
- **Brad Blanton,** *Radical Honesty* (1995)
- **Daniel Gilbert,** *Stumbling on Happiness* (2006)
- **Kristin Neff,** *Self-Compassion: The Proven Power of Being Kind to Yourself* (2011)
- **Carol Dweck,** *Mindset: The New Psychology of Success* (2006)
- **Angela Duckworth,** *Grit: The Power of Passion and Perseverance* (2016)

## PODCASTS

*Coached with Coach Keren Eldad (www.CoachKeren.com/podcast)*

*Expanded Podcast by To Be Magnetic (Law of Attraction)*

## MINDFULNESS TOOLS

**The Pause Principle:** A framework from *Gilded* that teaches the power of interrupting automatic reactions in moments of challenge. Instead of rushing to fix, fight, or flee, you "hit pause" and ask three questions:

1. Is the problem the main problem, or is my reaction about to make it bigger?

2. Is there another way to see this?

3. What is the opportunity here?

The Pause Principle creates space for wiser choices, alignment, and leadership grounded in clarity rather than reactivity.

**Byron Katie's The Work:** *https://thework.com*
**The Feelings Wheel:** *download here (free): https://feelingswheel.com/*

## ABOUT THE AUTHOR

A THOUGHT LEADER in the coaching world, Keren Eldad ("Coach Keren") specializes in taking high achievers out of the futility of constant pursuit and into the greatest levels of success and fulfillment. Her coaching clients include Olympic athletes, politicians, Hollywood stars, supermodels, Special Forces operatives, and serial entrepreneurs, as well as renowned global organizations such as Estée Lauder, J.P. Morgan, and Nike. She is also the founder of THE CLUB, a community of leaders, entrepreneurs, and coaches who encourage and support each other to reach their fullest potential and to make their greatest contribution.

Recognized as a Top Ten Executive Coach by the International Coaching Federation (ICF), *Real Leaders Magazine*, and Goop, Keren maintains gold-standard coaching credentials on top of her advanced academic degrees from the London School of Economics and the University of Jerusalem. She is also a former C-suite executive, who has lived and worked in seventeen countries and on four continents and now coaches leaders all around the globe in four languages: English, Spanish, Hebrew, and French. With half a million views on her TEDx talks and speaking engagements all over the world, Keren's message seems to transcend borders. She hopes it resonates with you.

Coach Keren resides in Austin, Texas, with her husband, Ryan, and many beloved pets. For booking and coaching consultations, contact Lee@ KerenEldad.com.